J. R. SPANGLER

And Remember—
JESUS IS COMING SOON

Compiled and edited by
John M. Fowler

Ministerial Association
General Conference of Seventh-day Adventists
Silver Spring, Maryland U.S.A.

PRINTED IN U.S.A.
by Pacific Press Publishing Association
Nampa, ID 83687

No project is the venture of a single person. This one, especially, is a joint venture. Special thanks to:

John M. Fowler who compiled and edited this book.
Harold D. Baasch who did the initial research.
Catherine L. Payne who coordinated production.
McKee Foods Corporation for sponsoring the development of this resource.

ISBN 1-57847-013-7

Table of Contents

Preface

Sudden, sad, and shocking.

Devastated by the news of the tragedy on a Los Angeles freeway that snapped the life of Bob Spangler on the morning of September 19, 1997, I called their home, to speak to someone, to whisper encouragement to whoever picked up the phone, or just to leave a message of concern. Instead, the voice on the machine, a voice that had proclaimed Jesus for nearly 54 years, had a message for me that left me stunned and challenged. The voice of Bob Spangler was clear: "Please leave your name and number at the beep and remember . . . Jesus is coming soon!"

Throughout his life and ministry, Bob identified himself with Jesus and the certainty and assurance that only Jesus can bring to life. Bob knew his Saviour personally, experientially, and proclamationally. Every talent he had—and Bob had a multitude of them—he, along with his wife, Marie, used for Jesus: to preach His good news, to offer hope to someone hurting, to raise up a church, to be a pastor of pastors everywhere, to write tirelessly on the meaning, message, and mission of Adventism.

Bob served 28 years in the Ministerial Association of the General Conference, both as its secretary, and also as editor of *Ministry* magazine for 23 years. Under his stewardship, *Ministry* became truly the pastor's professional journal, providing support to every aspect of pastoral ministry, including the creation of the Shepherdess ministry. Even more notable was his vision of taking *Ministry* to clergy of all denominations throughout the world through the PREACH program. The result has been astounding: ministers of other denominations and faiths have understood Adventism better and have come to appreciate our emphasis of "truth as it is in Jesus." And many have embraced that truth as well.

Bob had no hesitation at all in what he believed and Whom he served. Whether it was heading up the evangelistic rush to Russia as soon as the doors opened or publishing the popular *Seventh-day Adventists Believe* or raising funds for a church project that was dear to his heart, he knew his mission. And he had the vision to carry it through.

Even as he continually proclaimed, "Remember . . . Jesus is coming soon," those of us who heard him sensed an unquestionable certainty in his life, faith, and work. He knew his God. He knew his faith. He knew his church. He knew his calling.

In memory of this Adventist stalwart, the General Conference Ministerial Association presents this volume of the best of Bob Spangler's writings, with the hope that Bob's certainty of faith will also be our own.

—James A. Cress, Secretary
Ministerial Association, General Conference of Seventh-day Adventists
October, 1997

"Wisps of Glory"

Poet Maya Angelou could well have been describing Bob Spangler when she wrote of one who came "from the Creator . . . trailing wisps of glory."

Through Bob's ministry, "the glorious gospel of Christ" has shone on us and tens of thousands of others. Soon after I became president of the General Conference, I asked Bob to come to my office. I knew of his experience as a missionary in Asia. As a conference president, I had drawn on his services for camp meeting and workers' retreats, and I knew of his passion for souls.

"Bob," I said, "you are God's man to lead this church in evangelizing the Soviet Union. You won't have to go through any committees. You have my confidence and the confidence of your fellow church leaders. Just go to it. And come in now and then to tell me what I can do to help."

Much of the great evangelistic outreach throughout the former Soviet Union is the result of Bob's planning, organization, and fund raising. He had the gift to dream great dreams, to dare great deeds, and to get them done.

Even after retirement—in fact, one might say, especially after retirement—Bob raised hundreds of thousands of dollars for Russian projects, including the new Russian translation of the Scriptures, a tremendous achievement on its own. In the interests of Russian evangelism, Bob met with hundreds of *It is Written* partners, assisted with the annual fund raising, and coordinated the 1993 Moscow crusade conducted by Mark Finley. Indeed, Bob died on a Los Angeles freeway while in the service of *It Is Written.*

Because of another major contribution Bob made while editor of *Ministry* magazine, his work shall live on in hundreds of pulpits. I refer to the PREACH project, through which *Ministry* magazine has reached hundreds of thousands of ministers in all denominations. Today, in the United States alone, more than 100 of them now preach for us. And most trace their first acquaintance with the Adventist Church to reading the PREACH editions of *Ministry.*

Bob made another great contribution to this church: the publication of *Seventh-day Adventists Believe,* a readable, preachable volume on the 27 fundamental beliefs of the church. He not only published it but raised enough funds to distribute it gratis to more than 250,000 pastors and libraries.

In the Ministerial Association he was joined in service by his wife, Marie, who along with the late Ellen Bresee co-founded Shepherdess International to nurture pastoral spouses and families.

I believe with all my heart that the "wisp of glory" that trailed Bob Spangler throughout his earthly ministry shall be part of that "radiance splendid," for his witness ever brought glory to His Lord.

—Robert S. Folkenberg, President
General Conference of Seventh-day Adventists

Awaiting The Dawn

"Remember . . . Jesus is coming soon." Bob may not have been at home to answer the phone, but he made sure that his callers were greeted with the assurance that has ever been the consuming theme of his life and ministry.

Fifty-four years ago in Cleveland, Ohio, Elinor and I first met Marie and Bob. Elder R. A. Anderson was holding a citywide evangelistic campaign in the Masonic Temple on Euclid Avenue, and the four of us, among others, were a part of his team. Bob had just graduated from Columbia Union College and was a new ministerial intern. And I was completing my internship.

It was in Cleveland I saw Bob commit himself to being a preacher who would exalt nothing save Jesus Christ and Him crucified. During this time he determined to be a minister of righteousness by faith. He expressed a willingness to go as a missionary, and he made a covenant that the winning of souls to Christ was to be the focus of his life.

During our six months in Cleveland we developed a bond of friendship that, over time, became welded into a formidable relationship of mutuality and trust. It seemed we could discuss any matter without fear of being misunderstood or misjudged, and we could differ and still maintain the utmost regard for each other.

Then came a period of separation for 17 years while we both served the church in other challenging areas of the world. In God's providence it transpired that we were both called to the General Conference headquarters, where we spent 30 happy years as colleagues and fellow workers.

Fortuitously culminating all this, we found ourselves living next door to each other in adjoining town houses at Pitcairn Place in Burtonsville, Maryland, for more than 20 years. With only a wall between us, you can understand it was necessary to develop mutual compatibility which enriched and intensified our admiration and Christian love for one another.

Then, about four years ago, Bob and Marie seriously considered a move to California. Even though it was painful for us, we encouraged them, but only because it would mean they could be near their daughters, Patricia and Linda. Their move in no way weakened our friendship.

Even in death we seem to hear the fervency of Bob's voice affirming, "And remember . . . Jesus is coming soon." We shall now have to await that new dawn.

—Neal C. Wilson, Former President
General Conference of Seventh-day Adventists

Chapter 1

The Triune God

Have you ever used the phrase "not one iota of difference"? According to some this figure of speech has a rather important origin. It centers around Christ, Constantine, the church, a council, and a controversy.

A doctrinal dispute had led the Emperor Constantine to summon a general conference of the church at Nicaea in A.D. 325. The main debate was over the position of Christ in the Deity. Involved in this doctrinal struggle was the Greek letter "*iota*," which is the equivalent of our English "i." One religious faction became known as the Homoousians. They adhered to the belief that the Son of God is of the same essence or identical substance with the Father. A second rather large group of conservatives were labeled Homo*i*ousians. Their theory was that the Son is "essentially like" the Father but not of the same essence or substance.

The careful reader will note that the only difference between the spelling of these two words is the letter "i," in Greek an "iota." This seemingly small difference between the two words has led superficial thinkers to consider the whole affair a mere theological wrangle over nothing. Hence the expression, "not one iota of difference!" Referring to this debate, Thomas Carlyle, nineteenth-century Scottish essayist and historian, once sneered that "the Christian world was torn in pieces over a diphthong."

Yet the discerning Christian student knows that more than an "iota" or "diphthong" in the definition of the Deity is at stake. If Christ is fully God and the Holy Spirit is fully God, then the Godhead must be a trinity. Through the centuries untold numbers of minds have clashed over this point. Even today there are pockets of so-called Christians who will not accept the triune-God concept. Still, this truth furnished the key to all the essential doctrines of the Christian faith.

Beyond our ability to comprehend

One fact must be understood clearly by the seeker for truth. The nature and eternity of the Godhead is beyond our ability to comprehend. In these areas "The Omniscient One is above discussion."[1] How Father, Son, and Holy Spirit are three distinct personalities and yet one, how they are equal in power and authority and yet one, is beyond logic and reason. Perhaps those who doubt or deny the triune-God view are somewhat like the legendary single-cell amoeba who, on the basis of his own limited nature and being, declared that all other life must be confined to single-celled organisms. Imagine the shock of such an amoeba when he meets a worm or a snail—not to mention a fish, bird, or a human! So with those who attempt to reason out God's positive structure composed of three Persons, but remaining one God!

A simple illustration helped strengthen my faith in the doctrine of the triune God. As a high school physics lab assistant, I was always fascinated by the bottle of mercury on our stockroom shelf. How intriguing it was to place a drop of mercury (a liquid metal) in my hand and divide it into several parts and then unite it into one large drop again by merely cupping my hand. This shiny silver-white substance, whether divided or united, was always the same substance, the same consistency, and had the exact same qualities.

A chemist can take three drops of mercury and describe them scientifically. The same scientific description would fit perfectly if the three drops were merged into one. The *only* difference would be quantity. Let us imagine ourselves taking a drop of mercury and dividing it into three parts and then uniting them. Anyone seeing just the one drop could conclude there was only one drop. Yet, we would know that the one drop was composed of three drops, for we had just seen them separately. The point is that it can be three drops and yet one drop!

So with the Godhead. If it were possible scientifically to describe the Father, the same formula could be applied to the Son and the Holy Spirit. They are of the same essence. All possess the same qualities of unrestricted wisdom, unparalleled goodness, unmeasurable mercy, unlimited love, unsurpassed intelligence, unending power, and unbounded glory!

Scriptural evidence for the triad

A beautiful combination of an Old Testament and New Testament concept of the equality of Christ with the Father is found in Psalm 45:6 and Hebrews 1:8. "But unto the Son he saith, Thy throne, O God, is for ever and ever." Micah's prophecy of a coming Messiah claims for Him eternal pre-existence. He declared that Christ's "goings forth have been from of old, from everlasting" (Micah 5:2). Ellen White says, "From the days of eternity the Lord Jesus Christ was one with the Father."[2]

Undoubtedly, one of the most majestic passages of the Bible describing the deity of Christ is found in the writings of Isaiah. With an intensity of inspiration he ascribes to God the Son the attributes of God the Father. "For to us a child is born, to us a son is given; and the government will be upon his shoulder, and his name will be called 'Wonderful Counselor, Mighty God, Everlasting Father, Prince of Peace'" (Isa. 9:6, RSV). Could any statement be clearer than this to show that at least two members of the Trinity possess absolute oneness and equality?

New Testament evidence

Coming to the New Testament, we find that when Jesus was baptized the Spirit of God descended upon Him in the likeness of a dove. At the same time the Father declared His pleasure in His Son (Matt. 3:16, 17). All three Persons of the Godhead are shown in various actions at the baptism. Little wonder that

Augustine said to the heretics who doubted the triune God, "Go to the Jordan, and thou shalt see the Trinity."

The gospel commission commands surrendered souls to be baptized in the name of the Father, Son, and the Holy Ghost (Matt. 28:19, 20). The apostolic benediction lists the Three and names Christ first (2 Cor. 13:14). Paul usually places God the Father first, but here it is reversed. To me this signifies the interchangeableness of the members of the Godhead since they are one in action and purpose.

Note how Paul explains the sharing in the work of redemption by the divine Three. "For through him [Christ] we both have access by one Spirit unto the Father" (Eph. 2:18). What an interest the heavenly Trio has in the redemption of the human race!

The testimony of Christ makes it clear that each member of the Trinity possesses not partially but fully the same abilities and attributes. "I and my Father are one" (John 10:30). He said, "Believe me that I am in the Father, and the Father in me" (John 14:11). "I will not leave you comfortless: I will come to you [through the Spirit]" (John 14:18). Did you notice how Christ equates Himself with the Holy Spirit? "I will pray the Father, and he shall give you another Comforter, that he may abide with you for ever" (John 14:16). Surely the Holy Spirit cannot be inferior to Christ if He is to come in Christ's place. This promise of Christ implies the separate personality of the Spirit; otherwise this exchange of presence could not be possible.

The chief reason for Christ's daily trials and eventual death on the cross was not only because of His self-proclaimed Messiahship but was also due to His claim of equality with His Father. Hear His murderous accusers give reason for their attitudes when they declare that Christ "said . . . that God was his father, making himself equal with God" (John 5:18). Thus they "accused Him of blasphemy, showing that they understood Him as making this claim in the highest sense."[3]

Watch a small lad hugging his mother and saying, "I love you with my whole heart." Then watch him crawl into the lap of his father and whisper in his ears the very same words. Is it possible for him to have equal love for his two parents? Certainly! For a child to love his parents equally in no way diminishes his total love for them, but only enhances it. Could anyone reason that love for the mother alone is wholly adequate or at best is equal to the love that one could have for both mother and father? If this is true, then the child who is robbed of one of his parents through death or divorce really has not been deprived, suggesting that the family unit is meaningless.

So with the worshiper of the triune God. There is no divided allegiance, no partiality, when we reverence the Godhead. There is no jealousy on the part of the Trinity toward our actions. When we are in contact with the Holy Spirit we are in contact with God. When we contact Christ we are contacting the Spirit.

God is a jealous God, but He cannot be jealous of that which is a part of

Himself in essence, quality, and power. To worship the Holy Triad is no violation of the first commandment. When one subordinates his life and will to the ultimate unity of principle, purpose, and power of the triune God, it is never degrading. It is always, only elevating.

Increased self-worth

For one to believe Christ is any less God than the Father depreciates the meaning of His life and atonement. If someone not fully God died for me, then the impact of God's love for me would be decreased. The result—a devaluation of my own self-worth. This would automatically render me incapable of reaching my highest capacity of adoration and appreciation for God, who so loved me that He gave Himself through One equal with Himself to die in my place. Only God could reveal God fully. Only the death of one equal with God could satisfy the claims of the law.

If you had a dinner appointment with the President of the United States, how would you feel if, due to certain circumstances, a substitute would take his place? Even if the substitute were the vice-president, the impact of the invitation would be lessened.

But this is not true when communing with any of the Trinity. Whether it be the Father, the Son, or the Holy Spirit, fellowship with any one of these three is equally extraordinary.

Why do I believe in the triune God? God the Father gave His Son for me. God the Son died for me. God the Holy Spirit bends low to minister to me. This unified action has made it possible for me to be one with them forever.

---

[1]   *The Ministry of Healing,* p. 429
[2]   *The Desire of Ages,* p. 19
[3]   *Ibid.,* pp. 207-208.

Chapter 2

The One Altogether Lovely

Ellen White referred favorably to the writings of such seventeenth-century English dissenters as Baxter, Flavel, and Alleine, along with Bunyan. After having begun to read some of these books recently, it is a mystery to me why they were not required reading during my college and seminary days. We may not agree with every point of theology presented, but they are thoroughly saturated with Christ. If Adventists are to be foremost in uplifting Christ before the world,[1] we can certainly learn a few lessons in this by sitting at the feet of these men of God.

Christ-centered preaching

My memory still stabs me as I recall my limited concept of Christ-centered preaching during much of my ministry. My idea was to tack Christ onto my sermons and evangelistic discourses—usually at the end. This method never really satisfied me, but only in recent days have I had a deeper understanding of Christ-centered preaching. It might be an oversimplification of my new method to describe it as tacking doctrine, prophecy, or whatever onto an exposition of Jesus Christ and Him crucified, but what I am saying is that Christ must be exalted as the One "altogether lovely" (Song of Sol. 5:16). He must be first, last, and best in every sermon. We can set our hearts and eyes on no one lovelier. "Thou art fairer than the children of men" (Ps. 45:2).

As I read John Flavel's book, *The Method of Grace*, I am overwhelmed at the enormous wealth of his ideas and concepts on Jesus that he extracts from Scripture. Speaking of John Bunyan (1628-1688), Richard Baxter (1615-1691), Richard Alleine (1611-1681), and John Flavel (1630?-1691), Ellen White writes that these "and other men of talent, education, and deep Christian experience stood up in valiant defense of the faith which was once delivered to the saints. The work accomplished by these men, proscribed and outlawed by the rulers of this world, can never perish. Flavel's *Fountain of Life* and *Method of Grace* have taught thousands how to commit the keeping of their souls to Christ. Baxter's *Reformed Pastor* has proved a blessing to many who desire a revival of the work of God, and his *Saints' Everlasting Rest* has done its work in leading souls to the 'rest' that remaineth for the people of God."[2]

I strongly urge ministers to put their spiritual teeth into works of this nature. Today's religious writing, even the best, is often like pabulum compared with the thoughts expressed by these spiritual giants. You won't find many stories that yield short-term excitement, but you will find solid gospel meat that when chewed will become part of your spiritual bone and sinew. If anything is needful in today's problem-ridden and harassed society, it is a firm grasp of Jesus Christ such as these books provide. Sacrifice anything you must to buy and read these volumes of Puritan authors that "have taught thousands how to commit the keeping of their souls to Christ."

Permit me to share with you a few thoughts, some paraphrased, based on *The Method of Grace*. In the introduction Flavel writes, "It is the one thing needful for thee to get an assured interest in Jesus Christ; which being once obtained, thou mayest with boldness say, Come, troubles and distresses, losses and trials, prisons and death, I am prepared for you; do your worst, you can do me no harm; let the winds roar, the lightnings flash, the rain and hail fall never so furiously, I have a good roof over my head, a comfortable lodging provided for me: 'My place of defence is the munition of rocks, where bread shall be given me, and my water shall be sure'" (p. 9). Think what you may, but that paragraph beautifully expresses a concept some may hold but few practice.

An assured interest in Christ

How many of us have an "assured interest in Jesus Christ?" The term *assured* means "guaranteed," "certain," and "secure." How interested are we in Jesus? How real is He to us? What better way to waken our own drowsy conscience and those of this sleepy generation? If we be strangers to the person and work of Jesus, we commit the sin of making a powerless profession of Christ. If this be our condition, the scathing rebuke to Sardis is upon us—"a reputation of being alive, but you are dead" (Rev. 3:1, NIV). As Flavel so pointedly said, "How dangerous it is to be an old creature in the new creature's dress and habit" (p. 10).

In the final paragraph of his preface he movingly appeals: "One thing I earnestly request of all the people of God into whose hands this book shall fall, that they will be persuaded to end all the strifes among themselves which have wasted so much precious time and consumed the vital spirit of religion, hindered the conversion of multitudes, and increased and confirmed the atheism of the times. O put on, as the elect of God, bowels of mercy, and a spirit of charity and forbearance, if not for your own sakes, yet for the church's sake. O that you would dwell more in your closets, and be more frequently and fervently upon your knees: that you would search your hearts more narrowly and sift them more thoroughly than ever, before the Lord's fierce anger comes upon you: look into your Bibles, then into your hearts, and then to heaven, for true discovery of your condition" (pp. 11, 12). Should we not read this paragraph repeatedly?

Flavel's book uplifts Christ in a magnificent way. His chapter (a sermon, actually) "Christ Altogether Lovely" exudes the Saviour in every sentence. As all the rivers are gathered into the ocean, so Christ is the ocean in which all true delights and pleasures meet. In considering His person, His offices, His works, or anything belonging to Him, we see Him as the only One who is "altogether lovely." There is nothing unlovely in Him. "Thou art fairer than the children of men" (Ps. 45:2). The NIV states it, "You are the most excellent of men." Flavel makes the following points in weighing the expression "altogether lovely."

1. It excludes all unloveliness. Thus Jesus infinitely transcends the most excellent and lovely of creatures, for whatever loveliness is found in them is not without imperfection. The fairest pictures must have their shadows; the most transparent stones must have their polished metal or gold leaf placed under them to set off their beauty; the best creature is but bittersweet at best since there is always something displeasing alongside that which is pleasing. But not so with our Saviour, who is *altogether* lovely. His excellencies are pure and unmixed. He alone is a sea of sweetness without one drop of gall.

2. As nothing unlovely is to be found in Him, all that is in Him is wholly lovely. As every particle of gold is precious, so everything that is in Christ is precious. Who can weigh Christ in a pair of balances and tell His worth? His price is above rubies, and all that you can desire is not to be compared with Him (see Prov. 8:11).

3. He is comprehensive of all things lovely. He seals up the sum of all loveliness. Things that shine as single stars with a particular glory all meet in Christ as a glorious constellation. "For God was pleased to have all his fullness dwell in him" (Col. 1:19, NIV). Cast your eyes among all created beings, observe strength in one, beauty in a second, faithfulness in a third, wisdom in a fourth; but you shall find none excelling in them all as does Christ. He is bread to the hungry, water to the thirsty, a garment to the naked, healing to the wounded, and whatever a soul can desire is found in Him (see 1 Cor. 1:30).

4. Nothing is lovely in opposition to Him, or in separation from Him. Whatever is opposed to or separate from Him can have no loveliness in it. Take away Christ, and where is the loveliness of any enjoyment? The best creature comfort apart from Christ is but a broken cistern; it cannot hold one drop of true comfort (see Ps. 73:26). It is with the loveliest creatures as with a beautiful image in a mirror—turn away the face and where is the image? So, riches, honors, and comfortable relations are sweet when the face of Christ smiles upon us through them, but without Him what empty trifles are they all!

5. He transcends all created excellencies in beauty and loveliness. Compared to Christ, all other things pale, be they ever so lovely, ever so excellent and desirable. Christ carries away all loveliness from them. He is before all things (Col. 1:17), not only in time, nature, and order, but in dignity, glory, and true excellence. In all things He must have the preeminence.

All other loveliness is derivative and secondary, but the loveliness of Christ is original and primary. Angels and men, the world and all that is desirable in it, receive what excellence they have from Him. They are streams from the fountain. The loveliness and excellence of all other things is but relative, consisting in their reference to Christ and subservient to His glory. But Christ is lovely in Himself. He is desirable for Himself; other things are so because of Him.

The beauty and loveliness of all other things is perishing, but the loveliness of Christ is eternally fresh. The sweetness of the best of creatures is a fading flower; if not before, yet certainly at death it must fade away. "Doth not their excellency which is in them go away?" (Job 4:21). Yes, whether natural excellencies of the body, acquired endowments of the mind, lovely features, amiable qualities, attractive excellencies—all these like pleasant flowers are withered, defaced, and destroyed by death; but Christ is "the same yesterday, and today, and for ever" (Heb. 13:8).

The beauty and excellence of creatures is ensnaring and dangerous. A person may make them an idol and dote upon them beyond the bounds of moderation, but there is no danger of excess in love for Christ.

The loveliness of every creature is of a satiating nature. Our estimation of it abates and sinks by our nearer approach to it or longer enjoyment of it. Creatures, like pictures, are fairest at a due distance, but it is not so with Christ. The nearer the soul approaches Him, and the longer it lives in the enjoyment of Him, the more sweet and desirable He is to it.

All other loveliness proves unsatisfying to the human soul. There is not room enough in all created things for the soul to dilate and expatiate itself; it still feels itself confined and narrowed within those limits, like a ship in a narrow river that hath not room to turn and is ever and anon striking ground and foundering in the shallows. But Jesus Christ is in every way adequate to the vast desires of the soul; in Him a person has sea-room enough; there he or she may spread all the sails with no fear of touching the bottom.

These few thoughts are only a taste of Flavel's rich sermon on Jesus, the altogether lovely One. I trust this sample has whetted your appetite for more and more. I trust it will motivate us all to covet every moment possible for spending in His presence through study and meditation. Then with hearts filled and saturated with Him, we may lift Him up before the people. No other under heaven can save and satisfy our longings.

---

1   See *Gospel Workers*, p. 156.
2   *The Great Controversy*, pp. 252, 253.

Chapter 3

Why I Am a Creationist

Several years ago aboard a plane from Geneva to London, my seatmate and I began comparing beliefs. He, a philosopher-evolutionist, presented scientific evidence that he felt supported the theory of evolution, and I endeavored to show how the same evidence could be used in favor of creationism. I found that the most telling arguments in favor of creationism are not necessarily those that can be classified as scientific evidence. The facts are that both evolutionists and creationists employ arguments that are actually based on a very small amount of scientific evidence when compared to the whole realm that might be available. There is just not enough known data on either side to prove one position or the other scientifically and conclusively.

As a creationist, I take the Bible just as it reads and believe God created our world in seven literal 24-hour days. It is my firm conviction that scientific data, when viewed objectively, supports the simple Bible story just as well as, if not better than, the evolutionary theory. If one-tenth the amount of money and study that has gone into the development of the evolutionary theory had been put into the development of a scientific creationism there would be a more universal acceptance of the concept that the weight of evidence is on the side of special creation. However, I am convinced that the overwhelming advantage of the creationist's position lies in that which cannot be examined through the microscope or evaluated in the laboratory.

My discussion with my seatmate led into a look at the question of origins of life from a realistic, practical, personal angle. For instance, we discussed the emotional impact beliefs make on a person's happiness. People are creatures with strong emotions. Wars are fought, empires are built, culture is created, and even the human race is propagated more on emotion than any other element. Such emotions as love, fear, hate, and anger are extremely complex feelings that involve the mental and the physical qualities of the human. From the moment we are born to the moment we die we are either the victims or the beneficiaries of our emotions.

I recognize that the emotional factor is a reason why some evolutionists reject creationism. They contend that those who are not mature must lean on a belief in a superior being as a source of security. Thus, they say, only the strong can be evolutionists while the weak are creationists.

But I firmly believe that the creationist viewpoint does not impoverish man in the least. Does the evolutionist get more out of life than I do? Is life less meaningful to me? Is there greater purpose to the evolutionist's existence than to mine?

Would accepting the evolutionary theory make me a happier, more loving and lovable person? If I became an evolutionist would I have a greater or lesser degree of security? What advantages are mine as a creationist? These are certainly fair questions.

Having never been an evolutionist I recognize that I cannot fully understand the feelings or the point of view of the evolutionist. But I am well acquainted with individuals who have changed from evolutionists to creationists, and these unanimously vote in favor of the creationist's way of life. Accepting the scriptural account of Creation brings to us a most elevating and comforting thought. We are creatures made in God's image. He is our Father, and we are His children. A powerful impact is made on our minds when this concept is believed.

Where did the principle of love come from? It could not possibly have evolved! Furthermore, it is a most unnecessary element in the evolutionary theory. In what way could love be included in the process of vast eons of time?

A designer with love

The creation of life as we know it demands not only a designer but one with a personality of love. Thus, the principle of love is wrapped up in the Creation story. The creationist sees every manifestation of creative power as an expression of infinite love on the part of a personal God. Whether it be an atom of air or a giant galaxy of stars, infinite love is expressed through His created works. Believing this makes me a stronger person. It matures my attitude toward my fellow beings and gives me a greater appreciation for my neighbor.

Some years ago the United States was involved in the investigation of a leading citizen who was working as a spy for a foreign government that had eliminated from its political philosophy any concept of a supreme being called God. The former spy, after the trial was over, wrote of his transformation from an atheist to a believer in God and His creative power. One special incident started him on the road of belief. One day while eating with his family his eyes focused on his child's ear. As he looked at the intricate configuration of this seemingly insignificant part of the body, the thought struck him forcefully as to the impossibility of a human ear evolving over a long period of time without a personal designer. Then he reasoned that if an ear could not be produced through evolutionary processes, how could the more complex portions of the human anatomy evolve by chance? The obvious answer led him into a relationship with the Creator.

True happiness in life

When my emotions rise up as an overwhelming tide of joy when viewing a gorgeous sunset or when looking at a quiet countryside with its hills, streams, and forests, my mind can be lifted up in praise and gratitude to a Supreme Designer. What do atheists do when they see the same sights or when they hold their tiny infants tightly in their arms? What a leanness of soul must be theirs if they do not have the thrilling experience of letting their mind focus on the Creator-God who has given us every intellectual and artistic gift, every emotional capacity, and every gift of grace and love. Life is more than animal existence—life in its very essence is spiritual. True happiness in life is measured not by quantity but by quality, and the creationist view surely adds this latter dimension.

Another point to consider is the tremendous sense of security and self-worth bound up in this concept. With sociologists, psychologists, and psychiatrists attempting to help people experience some degree of self-worth, I suggest that they teach them the story of Creation. Security thrives on the creationist belief. When God made us in His own image, He wanted us—He needed people. It is impossible for me to understand how a true sense of security and dignity can exist outside an understanding that life has come into existence through God's creative power.

The promise of eternal existence

Finally, the promise of an eternal existence in a re-created perfect world is held out, not to creatures who have evolved from a near zero ancestor to what we are now, but to sons and daughters of Adam, who was the son of God. Christ sacrificed His life to redeem fallen humanity created in His own image, not that of noble beasts. Even if the whole story of redemption were a lie, I would rather order my life after the principles found in the Scriptures, which are far more elevating in concept than those found in the evolutionary theory. Only in the Scriptures is there held out to me life beyond the grave.

If we are just a meaningless cosmic accident, and if the evolutionists' goals consist of changing our world into an earthly heaven by political, social, and economic reforms, I ask on what basis do they hold out any hope of permanent success? Past history provides absolutely no evidence of any permanent change in human behavior through humanistic endeavors. But it does supply numerous examples of individuals who have changed for the better through a surrender to and acceptance of Jesus Christ as Lord and Saviour. Strange indeed that the altruistic motives of evolutionists who may work diligently to better human life should not lead them to a thorough consideration of God's plan revealed through the Scriptures. To provide humans now with a superior life involving their mental, physical, and spiritual capacities is the objective of God's plan.

But this plan goes far beyond our present existence, to eternal life in the future. True Christians can have their cake and eat it too—today, tomorrow, and forever! Those who in this life live according to God's plan certainly get more out of life than those who reject it. This, plus the additional insurance benefits of eternal life, never makes a person a loser, but a winner.

These are a few of the things my philosopher-evolutionist friend and I discussed while on the plane. When our conversation terminated he reached over and grasped my hand and while looking me straight in the eyes said, "I would give everything I own in life to believe as you do." Here was a man who wanted to believe in a Creator-God but couldn't. The seeds of doubt had been sown so deeply in that man's poor soul that he couldn't, at least at that point, rise above the miasma of unbelief to acceptance of a personal God who created the universe. My new friend, by his own admission, was a very depressed, discouraged individual. Could it be that his state of mind was to a great degree traceable to his evolutionary beliefs?

Chapter 4

You Must Be Born Again

The thousandth chapter of the Bible, John 3, should really have started with the last three verses of chapter 2. Jesus was in Jerusalem at the time of the Passover, and many believed on Him as they saw His miracles. But Jesus did not trust Himself and His work to them because He knew what men were like. In fact, "He knew men so well, all of them, that he needed no evidence from others about a man, for he himself could tell what was in a man" (verse 25, NEB). Chapter 3 proves this point with the experience of Nicodemus. A top leader of the church, who should have known the purpose for the church's existence, was ignorant of the ABC's of salvation. He may have been a qualified religious leader in financial affairs, social action, organization, and policy making, but he was illiterate regarding the one and only purpose for which the church exists.

Though talented, wealthy, educated, and honored, Nicodemus was in need of spiritual regeneration, but didn't consciously sense this need. He knew the Jewish nation needed a Messiah who would liberate them from the clutches of a heathen power. But what he didn't know was his personal need of a Messiah who would liberate him from the penalty and power of sin. A person may be ignorant of many things in the Scriptures and still be saved. On the other hand, one may be saturated with spiritual knowledge and yet be lost. Ignorance like that of Nicodemus is far too common among us as religious leaders today.

The first approach Christ's night school student used was one of flattery. Nicodemus accorded this Galilean peasant, who had no formal training, the honorable title "Rabbi." He topped this off by declaring Him "a teacher sent by God; [for] no one could perform these signs of yours unless God were with him" (John 3:2, NEB).

This remark indicates Nicodemus' thinking was wrong. His evaluation of Christ was based on His performance, not on who He was. His ignorance of Christ's mission limited him to calling Christ a teacher but not a Saviour. Imagine what would have happened if Peter had been with Christ that night. How his eyes would have sparkled with pride for his Master when this chief ruler began eulogizing, "You are a great teacher and miracle worker—Yours is a special relationship with God." What beautiful words, Peter muses. What an acknowledgment! Compare his attitude with the carpers who plague us daily. Nothing to date has been said by anyone comparable to this. Fantastic admission. The Master must be pleased. He searches Christ's face for signs of positive response. He sees neither anger nor charm, only love. But what he hears is astounding!

Christ forthrightly, yet kindly, tells His listener that he is lost unless a new birth is experienced. These words were shocking not only to Nicodemus but also would have been to Peter had he been there. Can't you see Peter leaning over and whispering excitedly, "Master, don't you know who this man is? Why, he is a leading member of the Sanhedrin. A wealthy, educated, highly respected, honorable, upright, and law-abiding citizen. Furthermore, he is a friendly neighbor, a fine husband, and father. He is a Sabbathkeeper, tithe payer, and his character and morals are impeccable. He is the kind of person the church desperately needs. Think of the prestige he will bring to our ranks. Imagine the influence of his act on others. Please, please, welcome him to our ranks, and I will make arrangements for his baptism tomorrow! Following that, I will arrange for a picture story to be published on the front page of the general church paper. Just imagine the headlines—Sanhedrin Member Baptized!"

Must be born again

Ignoring this imaginary advice, Christ makes the point even stronger in verse 7 as He bluntly informs Nicodemus, "Ye *must* be born again." There is something binding about that word "must." The word is nonnegotiable. It is "either/or"—no way around it. Those who do have a new-birth relationship wouldn't have it any other way. Compromise would be about as sane as a patient telling a surgeon to cut out his heart but spare his life. Life and heart are inseparable; so are the new birth and meaningful life!

Many people have no idea why Christ made such an unalterable demand on Nicodemus for entrance into eternal life. Verse 6 gives us an insight: "That which is born of the flesh is flesh." Christ here expresses a most unpopular truth.

Even if Nicodemus could enter his mother's womb and be born the second time, or ten times, or a thousand times, he still would be born a sinner. We are born with the seeds of sin in our being, bequeathed to us by Father Adam. Rear a baby in a sin-free atmosphere, and he or she will inevitably sin. If the whole human race were put in heaven today, this would not guarantee a stoppage of "evil thoughts, murders, adulteries, fornications, thefts, false witness, blasphemies" (Matt. 15:19). Sinners don't become saints just by environmental change. Living in heaven might modify a person's behavior a bit, but without a new-birth experience there would be no guarantee of a permanent change.

For this reason God asks the question about every soul, "What kind of chance would I take if I allowed this person into My kingdom?" That is a serious question everyone ought to think about, and it was a question Christ indirectly asked Nicodemus.

Complete transformation needed

I have often wondered what behavior therapists do with John 1:12, 13: "But as many as received him, to them gave he power to become the sons of God, even to them that believe on his name: which were born, not of blood, nor of the will of the flesh, nor of the will of man, but of God." The phrase "not of blood" had special significance to the Jews, who traced their noble lineage to Father Abraham. In a modern setting we are quite aware that "blue bloods" are just as capable of being prodigals as anyone else.

The next phrase, "nor of the will of the flesh, nor of the will of man," prophetically renders science quite powerless to permanently prepare humans for heavenly citizenship. Whether it be such techniques as shock therapy, brain surgery, behavior modification, chemotherapy, supportive psychotherapy, deep analytical psychotherapy, assertion training, rational-emotive techniques, psycho-dynamic or Freudian approaches, reciprocal inhibitions, systematic desensitiza-tion, operant conditioning, self-directed behavior modification programs, yoga, or transcendental medication, none can produce the new birth experience. We would not deny the usefulness of certain behavior modification techniques in aiding people to face life's stresses. One can stand all the improvement one can get by any legitimate means. But the new-birth experience is more than a patching up of the old life. It is a complete transformation!

The look of faith

Lest one get discouraged over this rather revolutionary concept, we find the Saviour explaining by what means it could be accomplished. Not only is the new birth a "must," but for its accomplishment we are obliged to obey a second "must." Christ shared with Nicodemus the secret of how a person is born again: "As Moses lifted up the serpent in the wilderness, even so *must* the Son of man be lifted up" (John 3:14). Here lies the genius of the new-birth experience. If an individual fails in finding and securing a conversion experience it is on this very point. He who fails in this area fails to lift up Christ in the wilderness of his heart. When Moses made a serpent of brass and elevated it high before the people, the gracious command was given that all who should look upon the serpent would live. Anybody who wanted to could look. Not that the brass serpent had power to help them, but it was a look of faith. It pointed to the One that was symbol-ized by the serpent, and that One was Christ.

Christ's revelation to Nicodemus unfolds an entirely new aspect of the atone-ment. Why didn't Moses lift up a lamb instead of a serpent? It is an amazing thought that God the Son came "in the likeness of sinful flesh" (Rom. 8:3). He identified himself with fallen humanity in order to lift us from the pit of sin and death to the highlands of salvation. The marvelous operation of the Holy Spirit, the third Person of the Godhead, is deeply involved in the transformation that takes place in the life of the individual who will look to Christ by faith alone. The venom of sin that has infected every person born into our world, the only excep-tion being Christ, can be neutralized by looking in faith to Him who knew no sin. Science cannot explain it. Discussion groups cannot fathom it. Reason cannot reason it. Only the one who looks by faith to Life will find life.

Reliance on works, obedience to God's law, or any other self-made plan for salvation spells eternal death! Nicodemus had difficulty in accepting this point. Little wonder that he exclaimed, "How can these things be?" A man of such integrity, morality, high principles, and good works found it almost beyond belief that he was a sinner in need of the pardoning grace of Jesus Christ.

When it comes to altering the deepest motives of a person's life, only an understanding of the atonement and a sense of Christ's pardoning love can effect any permanent change.

"The light shining from the cross reveals the love of God. His love is drawing us to Himself. If we do not resist this drawing, we shall be led to the foot of the cross in repentance for the sins that have crucified the Saviour. Then the Spirit of God through faith produces a new life in the soul. The thoughts and desires are brought into obedience to the will of Christ. The heart, the mind, are created anew in the image of Him who works in us to subdue all things to Himself. Then the law of God is written in the mind and heart, and we can say with Christ, 'I delight to do thy will, O my God.' Ps. 40:8."[1]

Lift the cross high

Fellow ministers, it is our responsibility and privilege to lift high the cross of Christ before our congregations. The cross should be the foundation of every sermon. It is a pledge of everlasting life. I am not talking about a cross that you put on a wall or hang around your neck, but the great principles of the atonement that are deeply branded upon the soul by the Holy Spirit. These alone can save and change men. God could reach more hearts and change more men if we would spend more time and effort on presenting the tremendous themes of Christ crucified, Christ resurrected, Christ ascended, Christ ministering in the heavenly sanctuary, and Christ coming again. Above all, let us preach Him from personal experience. If He is the living center of our lives He cannot help but be the center of our sermons.

When we share with others the preciousness of Christ and what He means to us, it will be as precious jewels that sparkle and shine in the brilliant sunlight. In this way sinners will be attracted to Him and not to ourselves.

What people, depressed people, people enslaved in destructive habits, people who are burdened with guilt, desperately need today is a new revelation of God's love that will lead to a new-birth experience.

"Ye must be born again."

---

[1]   *The Desire of Ages,* p. 176.

Chapter 5

Assurance Now

He had been a worker in the church for many years, Now retired, and seriously ill, he had requested prayer and anointing. As we gathered around the hospital bed, he told us the inner longing of his heart. His natural concern of healing was overridden by a deep concern for salvation. He urged that our prayers be not so much for physical restoration but for an increased ability to make fuller and deeper commitment to Jesus Christ. As he looked over his past life, the shortcomings and numerous failures brought an uncertainty into his mind as to whether the Lord had accepted him. His voice cracked and tears began to flow as he continued expressing hidden fears about the assurance of salvation.

Of course, only God has a correct and intimate knowledge of this heart. He alone knows the true record of this man's life. Those of us who knew him could only speak words of highest praise. His lifestyle, personality, and service commended him as one of God's true saints. His life was untainted with rebellion; his loyalty to Christ and His church was unquestioned. But somehow there was a misunderstanding of a most important facet of God's great plan of salvation. Such a misunderstanding is by no means peculiar to this dear Christian. I have come to believe seriously that a great many in our churches fail to understand fully the basis for God's acceptance of an individual for salvation. I believe this is one of the key points in the current discussions of righteousness by faith.

How God accepts sinners

I can testify that this truth, through the influence of the Holy Spirit, has come as a fresh new revelation to my own heart and life during the past several years. To me, the assurance of salvation is a precious truth that needs to be handled properly and with care. In this area, perhaps as in no other, misunderstanding is so easy and so fraught with disastrous results. The doctrine of salvation is not one that can be handled carelessly or foolishly; it is the most solemn matter for the human mind to consider. As we speak and write on such exalted themes, we must be ever careful to avoid exaggerated statements and far-fetched illustrations, for Satan will seize upon all such to distort God's truth and to perplex souls.

The subject of the assurance of salvation is one that our church has talked little about. The vast majority of our books and magazines say almost nothing about it. Most of the sermons that I have heard in my 35 years of ministry have never referred to it. And as a result there is much misunderstanding on the subject within the church—and much uncertainty regarding salvation.

The central point in an assurance of salvation is to be found in an understanding of the basis on which God accepts sinners. Looking back on my own personal experience, I have always understood that as a sinner I came to Christ without any merit of my own, totally in need of salvation. There was no question in my mind on that point. Ephesians 2:8, 9 said it plainly: "For by grace are ye saved through faith; and that not of yourselves: it is the gift of God: not of works, lest any man should boast." My sinful self deserves the death penalty. I have nothing by which to recommend myself to God. How often I have preached that point to thousands who have attended my evangelistic meetings! How often I have quoted during college weeks of prayer this statement from *Steps to Christ*: "How many there are who think they are not good enough to come to Christ" (p. 31). I have urged my listeners, "Come to Jesus just as you are." Remember the song "Just As I Am"? Beautiful, isn't it? So the basis of my acceptance with God, as I have always understood it, was solely the merits of Christ, not my merits. I believe all those within our church see eye to eye on this tremendous truth.

But what takes place *after* a person comes to Christ? Here is where I wish to center our thoughts. I knew and believed that a sinner, coming initially to Christ, must depend entirely upon the merits of the Saviour for acceptance. But now note the subtle switch. *After* coming to Christ and *after* starting on the road of sanctification, I based God's acceptance of me—consciously or unconsciously—partially or even wholly on *my performance*. I did not consider such an attitude as salvation by works. I still held that salvation is by faith alone. But recently I have begun to examine this subject carefully, and frankly I am convinced that my former opinion actually tied my acceptance by God and my assurance of salvation to my works—my performance.

I am aware that at this point the subject becomes quite slippery, easily leading to antinomianism and the idea that a man once saved is always saved. But such a perversion of the assurance of salvation need not be and will not be the case for those who are truly converted. It *will be* the case for those who love to cavil and argue. It *will be* the case for those who know nothing of the new-birth experience. It *will be* the case for those who can talk only about the cross and justification to the exclusion of sanctification—God's work of grace on the heart. It *will be* the case for those who are lovers of pleasure more than lovers of God. But we cannot and must not minimize or hold back this precious truth simply because there are those who will misinterpret and misuse God's plan of salvation to replace liberty with license. Correctly understood, this concept actually leads to *fuller* commitment to Christ.

Back to our point. Does the basis of my acceptance and assurance change after I come to Christ? Never! The basis of my acceptance and assurance is *and forever will be* the merits of Jesus Christ and never mine.

John Wesley's experience

The description of John Wesley's experience in this matter is helpful. Ellen White, in *The Great Controversy*, pages 255 and 256, summarizes Wesley's experience in the assurance of salvation. She describes how his encounter with some German Moravians aboard ship during a violent storm while crossing the Atlantic deeply impressed Wesley's mind. He admired the Christlike spirit of these people who gave continual proof of their humility in performing servant duties that the English refused. They helped others with no thought of remuneration, "saying it was good for their proud hearts, and their loving Saviour had done more for them" (p. 255). As Wesley observed their sweet spirit even when pushed, struck, or thrown down, he came to the conclusion that they had an experience with God that he knew nothing about. During the terrible storm, when most of the passengers were screaming and crying in terrible fear, the "Germans calmly sung on." Mystified, Wesley later asked whether they were afraid. The simple reply was, "No; our women and children are not afraid to die."

On Wesley's return to England, he came to a clearer understanding of Bible faith from a Moravian preacher. It was at this point that Wesley "was convinced that he must renounce all dependence upon his own works for salvation and must trust wholly to the 'Lamb of God, which taketh away the sin of the world.'"

Following this experience, he attended a Moravian meeting in London, where a statement was read from Luther, describing the change that the Spirit of God works in the heart of the believer. As Wesley listened, faith was kindled in his soul. "I felt my heart strangely warmed," he says. "I felt I did trust in Christ, Christ alone, for salvation; and an assurance was given me that He had taken away *my sins*, even *mine*, and saved *me* from the law of sin and death."

After reciting this thrilling episode, Ellen White describes Wesley's experience prior to his full conversion. As you read the next paragraph, perhaps you will see elements in his experience that have been repeated in your own or in that of some of your sheep. I fear that many of our precious people have gone, or are going, through a struggle similar to Wesley's.

"Through long years of wearisome and comfortless striving—years of rigorous self-denial, of reproach and humiliation—Wesley had steadfastly adhered to his one purpose of seeking God." Does this sound familiar? Here is a man who scrupulously obeyed every ray of light that came to him. But note that these were "long years of wearisome and comfortless striving."

Finally, Wesley had a profound conversion experience. "Now he had found Him [God]; and he found that the grace which he had toiled to win by prayers and fasts, by almsdeed and self-abnegation, was a gift, 'without money and without price.'"

Although I live the most rigid Christian life possible, including endless praying and fasting, plus the humbling of myself every minute of every day—none of it in any way merits salvation. In no way will such strivings influence my Lord to accept me as His child. I am His child through the merits of His Son alone, the Lord Jesus Christ. "Behold, what manner of love the Father hath bestowed upon us, that we should be called the sons of God" (1 John 3:1).

Are we called the sons of God because we merit it by our own good works? Never, never, never! Do we start the Christian life *by becoming* the sons of God through the merits of Jesus Christ and then switch *to remaining* sons of God because of our meritorious sanctified works? Never, never, never! Salvation begins with Christ and ends with Christ. Salvation is through grace by faith alone in Jesus Christ. Salvation is through grace by faith alone in Jesus Christ at the beginning, the middle, and the end of our Christian life span.

Ellen White, in continuing the account of Wesley's experience, makes the point unmistakably clear. "He continued his strict and self-denying life, not now as the *ground*, but the *result* of faith; not the *root*, but the *fruit* of holiness. The grace of God in Christ is the foundation of the Christian's hope, and that grace will be manifested in obedience. Wesley's life was devoted to the preaching of the great truths which he had received—justification through faith in the atoning blood of Christ, and the renewing power of the Holy Spirit upon the heart, bringing forth fruit in a life conformed to the example of Christ."

The result of faith, the fruit of holiness

Notice two important aspects of this paragraph. Wesley's assurance of salvation was based on the merits of Christ alone. This was the "grounds" and the "root" of his assurance. This point is one that needs to be clarified in the thinking of our people. If our sense of acceptance with God is based even partially on our performance, how can we possibly have the joy and gladness that should fill our soul? How can I, knowing and experiencing that the closer I come to Jesus, the more imperfections and defects I see in my own sinful self, ever have any shred of assurance of acceptance if my works form even part of God's basis for accepting me? If works, even sanctified works—the works Christ performs in me—are part of the reason God accepts me as His child, then how many works do I need before I can have assurance of being accepted? Or to put it another way, what level of sanctification must I reach before the Lord accepts me? Since sanctification is the work of a lifetime, and since I, as a Christian, should grow and mature spiritually on a daily basis, what point must I attain, even by His grace, to have the assurance of acceptance? This question is precisely what Wesley faced in his experience. It was precisely this uncertainty that made the years of his strivings so "wearisome and comfortless."

But there is a second important point to consider, and this is where many undiscerning followers of Christ can so easily be tripped. Note carefully that Wesley continued his strict and self-denying life "as the *result* of faith," the "*fruit of holiness*." Note the balance in the one sentence: "The grace of God in Christ is the foundation of the Christian's hope [justification], and that grace will be manifested in obedience [sanctification]."

"By their fruits ye shall know them," the Saviour warned (Matt. 7:20), and certainly the test holds true in this matter before us. What is the fruit of depending on Christ's righteousness for our assurance of salvation? Is it more devotion, greater spirituality, more faithful obedience? If so, we may be sure that we have correctly understood and appropriated the righteousness that comes solely by faith. Is the fruit carelessness in spiritual things, self-confidence, laxness in obeying God's will? Then we may be equally sure that we have not at all understood the righteousness that is by faith. Such an attitude is not righteousness by faith, but *unrighteousness by presumption.*

The apostle John cautions in blunt, unmistakable terms, "Let no man deceive you: he that doeth righteousness is righteous, even as he [Jesus Christ] is righteous" (1 John 3:7). It is not that those who *do* righteousness become righteous; rather, it is that those who *are* righteous through the merits of the Saviour alone will be doing righteousness. The test is still, "by their fruits ye shall know them." It is my conviction that if this point is understood as it should be there will be a latter-rain revival and a reformation in our midst that this church has never experienced. With our assurance of salvation established upon the merits of Christ alone, like Wesley, our souls will burn with the desire to carry the glorious gospel of God's free grace to everyone.

One of the greatest hindrances to our entire evangelistic outreach is, I feel, a lack of assurance on the part of our people. How can we share our faith in Christ unless we *know* that God has accepted us as His son or daughter? And how can we know we are His children unless we base our acceptance solely on Christ's merits alone? This is the foundation on which our love for Christ and motivation for His service are built.

How can anyone lower standards when the Holy Spirit presses this concept home to the mind? How can a person nurture the lust of the flesh and at the same time claim this assurance? How can anyone flaunt the grace and mercy of God by willfully walking in the muddy ruts of sin, when he understands that his hope is based on the merits of One who willingly went to the cross to make it possible for him to be accepted? Such a person is the victim of a strong delusion.

Listen to these soul-stirring words from Ellen White: "Hanging upon the cross Christ was the gospel. Now we have a message, 'Behold the Lamb of God, which taketh away the sins of the world.' Will not our church members keep their eyes fixed on a crucified and risen Saviour, in whom their hopes of eternal life are centered? This is our message, our argument, our doctrine, our warning to the impenitent, our encouragement for the sorrowing, the hope for every believer. If we can awaken an interest in men's minds that will cause them to fix their eyes on Christ, we may step aside, and ask them only to continue to fix their eyes upon the Lamb of God. They thus receive their lesson. Whosoever will come after Me, let him deny himself, and take up his cross, and follow Me. He whose eyes are fixed on Jesus will leave all. He will die to selfishness. He will believe in all the Word of God, which is so gloriously and wonderfully exalted in Christ."

"As the sinner sees Jesus as He is, an all-compassionate Saviour, hope and assurance take possession of his soul. The helpless soul is cast without any reservation upon Jesus. None can bear away from the vision of Christ Jesus crucified a lingering doubt. Unbelief is gone."[1]

"Not the labors of my hands
Can fulfill Thy law's demands;
Could my zeal no respite know,
Could my tears forever flow,
All for sin could not atone;
Thou must save, and Thou alone.

"Nothing in my hand I bring,
Simply to Thy cross I cling;
Naked, come to Thee for dress,
Helpless, look to Thee for grace;
Foul, I to the fountain fly;
Wash me, Saviour, or I die."

The importance of sanctification

But let me make it abundantly clear that our acceptance with God and our assurance of salvation, based as it is upon the merits of Jesus Christ, must not lead us to believe that works or sanctification are of little consequence. Faith and works must ever be kept in perspective. By that I mean the individual whose heart has been convicted by the Holy Spirit, and who is led to repentance and a new-birth experience, will respond with wholehearted obedience to the will of God as he or she understands it. It is unfortunate, indeed, that the glorious truth of salvation through the merits of Christ alone is blurred, and even downgraded at times, by the unwise illustrations and remarks of a few who claim to be advocates of salvation by faith alone in Jesus Christ.

For instance, one sincere soul claimed that although she couldn't keep from committing sin even for five minutes, she still had the assurance of salvation on the merits of Christ alone. This statement puzzles me. If taken one way, a non-Christian could ask, "What kind of a Saviour do you have? If you receive no benefits in terms of victory over evil, why become a Christian?" Of course, some professed Christians would agree with this statement, saying, "That's the beauty of it all. No matter what we do, we're still saved." This relegates the plan of salvation, it seems to me, to a ridiculous sublimity certainly unsupported by Scripture.

On the other hand, if this dear soul was distinguishing between an overt act of sin and a sinful state of being, she could have a point, although very poorly expressed.

My understanding of the nature of man is that he is born with a fallen nature. There is an antagonistic power resident in man. "There is in his nature a bent to evil, a force which, unaided, he cannot resist."[2] That force, stronger in some individuals than in others, is with us from birth until death. Paul declared, "For I know that nothing good dwells within me, that is, in my flesh" (Rom. 7:18, RSV). To further expand this point, may I refer to the words of Jeremiah 17:9: "The heart is deceitful above all things, and desperately wicked: who can know it?" Is the deceitfulness of the heart forever and totally eradicated at conversion? Was the publican's sinful nature eradicated after he cried out, "God be merciful to me a sinner," and went down to his house justified? His carnal nature was still existent, and quite capable of being revived at a moment's notice.

Advancing in Christian life

This is not to say that the born-again Christian will not be advancing in the Christian life. Never! The ultimate purpose of God's plan of salvation is to bring the human into complete harmony with the principles of His law, His character. The surrendering of the life to Jesus Christ is a surrender to a radical change of heart and reformation of life. There is no make-believe in this transformation! While I have stressed the imperfect state of the human, even following conversion, the Scriptures make it clear, abundantly clear, that we have a Saviour who is able to save us from the power of sin. If a person is not affected by what the Lord has done in His gracious act of forgiveness and justification, that person has a perverted understanding of the gospel.

One of my favorite parables is found in Matthew 18:21-35. Perhaps the importance of the truth contained in this parable is underlined by the tragic conclusion. It is the story of a servant who owed a multimillion-dollar debt to the king. When found out, he fell down at the king's feet and begged for mercy, saying, "Lord, have patience with me, and I will pay thee all" (verse 26). What an illustration of human desire to justify oneself with one's own works! Verse 25 makes it clear that he had absolutely nothing with which to pay, yet he promises to make good this enormous sum, which was equal to more than the entire revenue of Palestine during the days of Christ. The servant had no sense of the magnitude of his debt nor of the impossibility of ever satisfying it, or he never would have promised to pay it all back. Anything he could have paid would be infinitesimal compared with the total liability.

The amazing mercy of the Lord is noted in verse 27. He "loosed him, and forgave him the debt." Not only did he take away the prison sentence but he canceled the debt, as well. What a picture of our Lord's amazing grace! In tenderest love He cancels the debt of the sinner who, in repentance, begs for mercy.

But the story doesn't end with the glorious action of forgiveness! Forgiveness must produce a response of responsibility. This was what was lacking in the heart of the servant. After being forgiven a multimillion-dollar debt, he went out and found a fellow servant who owed him a pittance. The one who had been so mercifully treated, instead of demonstrating a corresponding mercy, "laid hands on him, and took him by the throat, saying, 'Pay me that thou owest'" (verse 28). What a distressing attitude! Furthermore, this ill-treated fellow servant fell down at his feet and asked for the same mercy that the forgiven one had so recently craved, and in the same words that the servant himself had used—but to no avail.

The lessons of this parable are clear and vivid. The first servant had no concept of the enormity of his debt. Furthermore, when he was forgiven he had no adequate realization of the mercy and graciousness of the Lord. His heart was not touched or humbled. He had no conversion experience. The new birth was unknown to him. If he was baptized at that point, he was buried alive, for self never died. He never arose to walk in the newness of life in Christ. In all probability, there was a superficial ecstasy, a shallow burst of appreciation, a shouting of "I am saved," but no real change of heart. Had he sensed that he owed everything to God's free grace, would he not have shown it in a sanctified life?

As Ellen White so beautifully expressed it, "We ourselves owe everything to God's free grace. Grace in the covenant ordained our adoption. Grace in the Saviour effected our redemption, our regeneration, and our exaltation to heirship with Christ. Let this grace be revealed to others."[3]

Lift up Christ!

I plead with my fellow ministers to lift up Christ more beautifully and clearly before the people. This will inevitably lift the standards of our people. I plead with you not to put the cart before the horse. Both the horse and the cart are important! But put them in the right order. If we hammer on standards, if we spend more time preaching the law than we do Christ, we will end up lowering the standards. Preach against sin, but show what it is in the light of the cross.

I ask you, in all honesty and sincerity, as you look at the church today, Are we stronger morally than ever before? Is the lifestyle of our members more like that of Jesus Christ than ever before? Is the character of Jesus shining through the lives of our church members in a more dramatic way than ever before? Are we more zealous in proclaiming the gospel? I don't know what your answer is, but I know what mine is. And I firmly believe that the main reason for our condition is because we have not properly lifted up Jesus before the people.

The admonition written scores of years ago is still valid today. "Of all professing Christians, Seventh-day Adventists should be foremost in uplifting Christ before the world."[4] What does this mean? Of all people in the world, we have had an amazing degree of light shining upon us through the Scriptures and the Spirit of Prophecy. No group on earth has ever had such detailed information regarding all phases of lifestyle. Furthermore, we believe that our movement constitutes the climax of the Protestant Reformation. This Reformation reaches its zenith in a people described symbolically as the 144,000, who are an undefiled group, with mouths uttering no guile, and who stand without fault before the throne of God (see Rev. 14:1-5). Are we anywhere near this state in our spiritual advancement? If not, why not?

I come back again to uplifting Christ. Spend more time in your sermons uplifting Him and His free grace. This will help the people to lay hold of His power to save. Only as we behold Him will divine transformations take place in the character. Direct your mind and the minds of your people to "the Lamb of God, which taketh away the sin of the world" (John 1:29). It is a deeper understanding of the life and the atonement of Jesus Christ that causes a flood of divine compassion to flow into our souls, which in turns transforms us. Focusing time and attention on the light bulb separated from the socket doesn't make light. But connect that light with the source of power and things change.

O preacher, spend time with Christ through His Word. Then let Christ and His goodness, His love and sacrifice, be the theme of your sermons. "Nothing can take so strong a hold on the heart as the abiding sense of our responsibility to God. Nothing reaches so fully down to the deepest motives of conduct as a sense of the pardoning love of Christ."[5]

1   Ellen G. White's comments on Gal. 6:14 in *The SDA Bible Commentary*.
2   *Education,* p. 29.
3   *Christ's Object Lessons*, p. 250.
4   *Gospel Workers,* p. 156.
5   *The Desire of Ages*, p. 493.

Chapter 6

Law and Grace

How can Seventh-day Adventists preach about God's grace and at the same time be so legalistic as to keep the Seventh-day Sabbath?

Are we legalists—people who ignore the central gospel truth of salvation by grace through faith in Jesus Christ? Undoubtedly the single most common misunderstanding about Seventh-day Adventists is the assumption that we teach salvation by the works of the law. Others have believed that we mix law and grace, depending partially on each for salvation.

I am first to admit that Adventists themselves have had a part to play in these misunderstandings. Too often Adventist publications and preaching have sounded legalistic because of the emphasis given to the importance of obeying God's law. When the Adventist Church arose in the mid-nineteenth century, most Christians shared a common belief in the unquestioned authority of God's law. It was natural for Adventists to place great stress on this mutual ground in presenting what they believed to be a recovery of a long-neglected truth—the seventh-day Sabbath. Yet the fact is that the Seventh-day Adventist Church has always firmly believed in salvation by grace through faith in Jesus Christ alone.

Actually, the relationship between law and grace can be clarified quickly if we answer a single question: Is the law of God (meaning the Ten Commandments) a standard of right and wrong, or is it a method of salvation? If the law is used as a method for salvation, then law and grace are as far apart as the east is from the west. But if the law is used as a standard of right and wrong, then law and grace fit together beautifully and as closely as the forefinger and thumb. A correct understanding of the relationship between law and grace will show that both are as important to spiritual life as are the heart and brain to physical life. Both are absolutely indispensable.

God's plan for salvation

This brings us to consider whether God's plan of salvation was different during Old Testament times from what it was in New Testament times. In Job, one of the earliest books in Scripture, the question is asked, "how then can man be justified with God?" (Job 25:4). From Genesis to Revelation one finds a unity of thought declaring that there can be no other provision for justification except Jesus Christ and His shed blood. The Old Testament system of sacrificial types simply pointed forward to Christ's sacrifice. Just prior to His death Jesus declared, "This is my blood of the covenant, which is poured out for many for the forgiveness of sins" (Matt. 26:28, RSV). God did not institute a plan of salvation by faith *after* the cross.

The entire sanctuary system taught the blood atonement of a coming Messiah.

From the first lamb offered by Adam and Eve to the last animal slain before Christ cried out on the cross, "It is finished," the theme of the sacrificial arrangement was "without the shedding of blood there is no forgiveness of sins" (Heb. 9:22, RSV). "It is the blood that makes atonement" (Lev. 17:11, RSV) was the Lord's instruction to Moses.

God's plan for dealing with sin became operative as soon as transgression occurred in Eden. The explanation of that plan began immediately, as well, and progressed through the years from the simple altars of the patriarchs to the time when God gave a fuller picture in the sacrificial ritual provided for the children of Israel. Every part of the sanctuary building and services was deeply significant. Daily, the ministration of the tabernacle taught the people the great truths concerning Christ's death.

The correct relationship between law and grace was illustrated in the ark of the covenant, placed in the Holy of Holies of the Old Testament sanctuary. Inside the ark was enshrined the law of God, written by His own finger, while covering the sacred chest was the mercy seat. The two golden cherubim at each end of the mercy seat had their faces turned toward each other looking downward, signifying their respect for the holy law and the mercy seat. Thus in the heart of the sanctuary "mercy and truth are met together; righteousness and peace have kissed each other" (Ps. 85:10). What a beautiful illustration of the relationship between law and grace!

Thus the Scriptures clearly indicate that salvation in the Old Testament was of grace through faith in a Saviour. True, many then, as now, perverted God's gracious plan into a system of earning salvation by works, but they did so contrary to the will of God (see Isaiah 1:10-20). Any claim that God changed His method of salvation after the cross is definitely unscriptural. One might well ask, "If one could be saved before the cross by works, why did God then change His plan to one of grace after the cross—a plan that required the suffering and death of His own Son?" Not a single scripture can be cited to show that between the time of Adam and John the Baptist an individual was saved by works. Whether Abraham or Amos, Paul or Peter, the sinner's right to the kingdom is based on faith in the Messiah, Jesus Christ.

Undoubtedly those living in Old Testament times did not have the great advantage of studying the atonement from a historical stance, as we do. But, though sometimes dimly perceived, God's method of salvation was still the same. Paul's declaration that God "hath chosen us in him before the foundation of the world" (Eph. 1:4) refers to all people living before and after the cross. The precious "Lamb slain from the foundation of the world" (Rev. 13:8) shed His blood for every person who has lived, from the days of the first Adam until the day when the second Adam shall appear in the clouds of heaven. God is a consistent God. "Jesus Christ is the same yesterday and today and for ever" (Heb. 13:8, RSV).

Teaching the plan of salvation

One major difference between the Old Testament and the New Testament is in God's *method* of teaching the plan of salvation. Teachers may use different methods of explaining that two plus two equals four, but the answer always remains the same. So God used a "kindergarten" method of symbols and sacrifices in explaining His plan of salvation to those who had not the privilege of seeing the reality of Calvary. Naturally, this method of teaching by types and shadows ended at the cross. Since that time, God's instruction in the ways of salvation has been more direct, but His plan is still the same.

The system of ceremonies and laws dealing with the sacrifices met its fulfillment in Christ and His death. But we cannot and dare not confuse these temporary laws with the eternal moral law of Ten Commandments. The entire life of Christ on earth exalted this eternal law of His Father. It existed before the creation of earth or man and will continue to exist as long as God Himself. Far from being a temporary shadow of things to come, the Ten-commandment law is so permanent that God could not possibly alter a single sentence in order to save us. That law is the foundation of His government—His unchangeable, eternal, infinite constitution, by which the universe is governed.

How *could* the plan of salvation be changed? Sin and its penalty have not changed. Stealing is sin, whether a person stole in 1978 B.C. or in A.D. 1978. Interestingly, charges of legalism almost always come in reference to the fourth commandment—Sabbathkeeping. Almost never is one accused of legalism for obedience to the commandments forbidding stealing, adultery, lying, or idol worship, in spite of the fact that one can just as easily be a legalist in these areas as in Sabbathkeeping. It should be obvious, as well, that one may be obedient to the commandment requiring Sabbath observance without being a legalist. The real question, therefore, must be this: Is the fourth commandment an integral, binding part of the eternal Ten-commandment law of God? If it is, obedience is not necessarily legalism, but disobedience is unmistakably sin.

Law and sin

In Old Testament times sin was tied to the violation of God's commandments. Nehemiah clearly states, "We have sinned against thee. . . . We have acted very corruptly against thee, and have not kept the commandments, the statutes, and the ordinances" (Neh. 1:6, 7, RSV). Jeremiah 44:23 connects sin with disobedience to God's law. A clear statement of what sin is can be found in the book of Leviticus: "If any one sins, doing any of the things which the Lord has commanded not to be done . . ." (chap. 5:17, RSV).

Coming to the New Testament, we find the definition of sin unmistakably clear. "Sin is the transgression of the law" (1 John 3:4). "For by the law is the knowledge of sin" (Rom. 3:20). "I had not known sin, but by the law: for I had not known lust, except the law had said, Thou shalt not covet" (Rom. 7:7). "For where no law is, there is no transgression" (Rom. 4:15). "But sin is not imputed when there is no law" (Rom. 5:13). "The strength of sin is the law" (1 Cor. 15:56). The point is that sin cannot be defined except in terms of the law. And the violation of the law cannot be defined except as sin.

Sin, the breaking of the law, began in Eden. "Wherefore, as by one man sin entered into the world, and death by sin; and so death passed upon all men, for that all have sinned" (Rom. 5:12). Paul emphasizes the point in another passage when he claims that "all have sinned" (Rom. 3:23), and because of this, "death passed upon all men," for "the wages of sin is death" (Rom. 5:12; 6:23).

The death penalty is not arbitrary. For God to remain true to His character, which, in a definite sense, is expressed in the law, He has no choice other than to invoke the death penalty upon those who rebel against His will. Otherwise His law, the entire foundational constitution of His government, would be threatened, His authority would be challenged, and ultimately the entire universe would be in as chaotic a condition as our present world. God has no choice—in order to maintain peace, liberty, and harmony throughout the universe—other than to take back His life from those whom He has created who rebel and refuse to obey His law.

Keep this point clearly in mind when you read, "By the deeds of the law there shall no flesh be justified in his sight." "Therefore we conclude that a man is justified by faith without the deeds of the law" (Rom. 3:20, 28). The reason no person can be justified by works of the law is that the penalty for transgressing the law is *death*, not works. A man who is sent to prison for 10 years walks out a free man after serving his sentence. He has paid the penalty and now stands justified in the presence of the law. This is justification by *works*. But if a man has committed a crime that requires the death penalty, would he be justified by serving 10 years, 20 years, or even 50 years? No amount of works would justify him; only death would satisfy the penalty. For this reason the Christian can never be made right with God on the basis of anything that *he or she* can do.

To try to justify ourselves by our works is even worse than impossible; it tremendously reduces in our minds the enormity of sin. If there is *any* work that I can perform to pay for the violation of any of God's commandments, then the removal of the penalty becomes a mere human effort. The real magnitude of sin becomes apparent only in the light of its penalty—death. But even greater than *my* death demanded by the law to deal with my sin is the staggering fact of *Jesus'* death to save me. That the sinless Lamb of God would willingly come to suffer the unspeakable agonies of my guilt and voluntarily bear my sin-caused death defies comprehension and demonstrates, as nothing else possibly can, the malignity of sin and the enduring holiness of God's law. All this is seen in the radiance streaming from the cross.

The relationship of law and grace

No wonder, when Paul concludes in Romans 3:28 that "a man is justified by faith without the deeds of the law," he goes on to ask the question, "Do we then make void the law through faith? God forbid: yea, we establish the law" (verse 31). Paul's statement gives us deep insight into the relationship of law and grace.

Seventh-day Adventists tenaciously hold to the doctrine of justification by faith alone, while at the same time pointing out the subtle error that the cross has abolished God's law, freeing the Christian from its claims. As the apostle Paul affirms, nothing could be farther from the truth.

Calvary is an eternal argument that God's law is as unchangeable as His character—as unchangeable as His throne—as unchangeable as His love. When our Saviour pleaded with the Father in Gethsemane to spare Him from drinking the cup of death, the only answer He received was the immutability of the sacred law. Death is the penalty for transgression. If salvation was to become reality, Christ must die, not for Himself, but for the transgressors of that law, including me. The fact that no other way could be found even by God Himself to satisfy the claims of the law is supreme proof of its eternal, unchangeable character. Would God have given His Son to die in order to redeem sinners from the penalty of the law if any other way could have been found? If God could have altered His law or its penalty, surely He would have done so!

How then can we behold the sacrifice upon the cross and at the same time ridicule the law He died to uphold? The cross, rightly comprehended, leads us to a true understanding of the terribleness of sin, which is the transgression of that law. The cross causes us as sinners to cry out for faith to lay hold of the merits of Christ and to cease from breaking that law.

The thought that Christ's death brought about the end of obedience to the law is blasphemy. This is why Paul cries out, "Does faith in Christ do away with the law?—God forbid, yea it establishes the law."

As Seventh-day Adventist ministers and Christians, we daily pray for power to overcome greed, thoughts of immorality, selfishness, and sin of every hue— not primarily for the harmony with Heaven this brings to us, but because of the knowledge of what our sins cost Heaven to forgive. To be canceled, our sins demand either our death or the death of our Creator.

How can Christians downgrade the law of God? Look at the center cross of the three on Mount Calvary. See the agony suffered by One who knew no sin. See Him whose tender skin as a baby was pricked with the straw in the manger now enduring the stabs of sharp thorns piercing His brow. See the rough spikes, made to hold one board tightly to another, now holding human flesh against a cross, piercing His hands and feet. Watch a soldier thrust a metal spear into His side. Why? Why? Why did Christ suffer all this?

No other way

The Saviour was willing because in no other way could sin be eradicated, and sin is the one thing in all the universe that God hates. We see glimpses of the misery caused by sin, but God sees it in all its enormity. Imagine His great heart of love twisted in pain at the sight of a world filled with His children who must endure the unrelenting onslaught of sin's crippling, emaciating destruction. Watch with Him the effects of sin—the widow weeping over her murdered husband, the heartaches of the lonely and forgotten, the physical and emotional scarring of the battered child, the starving millions, the drunkard careening his car into the bodies of innocent families. We can capture a fragment, but God has to view it all in the blinding noonday of omniscience.

Because it was unthinkable to God to allow sin to continue unchecked, and because the only way to destroy it was to accept its consequences personally, Jesus willingly went to the cross. The law demanded death for the transgressor as the only appropriate, adequate penalty. To demand less would reduce the importance of the law and permit sin to reign eternally.

It is not a question, really, of law *or* grace. Rather it is a question of law *and* grace. God's grace is based upon His law; His law forms the foundation upon which His grace is built.

Let us rejoice with all of heaven in God's free grace, which releases us from having to pay the penalty of our transgressions of His law. And let us with all of heaven rejoice that having been saved by His grace, we may freely follow His law by that same grace.

Chapter 7

The Subtle Deception of Works

Every now and then we as Christians need to examine the motivations behind our good works. The heart, according to Jeremiah, "is deceitful above all things, and desperately wicked." Furthermore, "who can know it?" (Jer. 17:9). It is not difficult for Christians to slip into the slime of salvation by works.

The apostle Paul labels meritorious works in the Christian life "rubbish." His desire was to "be found in him [Christ], not having a righteousness of my own that comes from the law, but that which is through faith in Christ—the righteousness that comes from God and is by faith" (Phil. 3:8, 9, NIV).

Peter is clear that we are not redeemed "with perishable things such as silver or gold . . . but with the precious blood of Christ, a lamb without blemish or defect" (1 Pet. 1:18, 19, NIV). These and other passages make it clear that neither sacraments, pilgrimages, baptism, commandment keeping, penance, confession, gifts to the church, candle burning, faithful church attendance, assisting the poor and needy, or any other good work will ever help merit salvation!

Paul, in his letter to Titus, which deals in part with the problem of Jewish legalism, speaks of the "kindness of God our Savior . . . for mankind." Then he declares that "He saved us, not on the basis of deeds which we have done in righteousness, but according to His mercy" (Titus 3:4, 5, NASB). The pure principles of the gospel found in the Scriptures in both the Old and New Testament make it clear that our salvation and acceptance by God is based not on our obedience, but on Christ's, for "by one Man's obedience many will be made righteous" (Rom. 5:19, NKJV). This obedience is available to believers who are "justified freely by his grace" (Rom. 3:24).

Justified by faith alone

How many believe that their standing before God does not depend on their good and bad deeds? Addressing this point Paul emphasizes that we are justified through faith by God's grace, not by works of the law. He points to Abraham, who "believed God and it was counted ["credited," NIV] unto him for righteousness" (Rom. 4:3; see also Gen. 15:6). He was justified before he underwent circumcision, not on account of it (Rom. 4:9, 10).

What kind of faith did Abraham have? The Scriptures reveal that "by faith Abraham obeyed" when God called him, leaving his homeland and traveling, "not knowing where he was going" (Heb. 11:8, NKJV; see also Gen. 12:4; 13:18). It is evident that Abraham had a genuine, living faith in God. And his faith was demonstrated by obedience. But his works of obedience never were meritorious, never recommended him to God, never paid for or helped pay for a single sin.

Tragically, the entire sacrificial system of the ancient Old Testament sanctuary was turned into a system of works. This perversion of the true gospel became so nauseating to God that He proclaimed through the prophet Isaiah: "The multitude of your sacrifices—what are they to me? . . . I have more than enough of burnt offerings, of rams and the fat of fattened animals; I have no pleasure in the blood of bulls and rams and goats. . . . Stop bringing meaningless offerings! Your incense is detestable to me. New moons, Sabbaths and convocations—I cannot bear your evil assemblies" (Isa. 1:11-14, NIV). Finally the Lord made this mighty appeal: "Come now, let us reason together. . . . Though your sins are like scarlet, they shall be as white as snow; though they are red as crimson, they shall be like wool" (Isa. 1:18, NIV).

Saved by Christ's merits

How does a person become clean, justified, and saved? On what basis are we accepted by God? It is through the merits of Christ alone. Nothing we do or ever can do will recommend us to God. God's justification of the sinner rests not on what the sinner does. Even if a person has a perfect character and renders absolute obedience, his justification is based on Christ's act of righteousness (see Rom. 5:18, 19).

Some pervert this tremendous truth by going to the opposite extreme. They ignore works entirely. Works done to earn merit should be ignored, but we cannot ignore the response of a Christ-loving Christian who senses God's tremendous love. We understand that while we have been "without strength," "ungodly," "sinners," and "enemies," God "commendeth his love toward us" (Rom. 5:6-10). This irresistible, unfathomable, incomprehensible love is what changes a person—is what converts a person. When we concentrate on God's magnificent love, not sporadically, but consistently, the Holy Spirit creates in our hearts an unconquerable desire to obey and serve Him. Like Paul at his Damascus road conversion experience, we cry out, "Lord, what do You want me to do?" But this response and our activities are founded on love, not on a desire to earn merit.

It is time for Christians of all persuasions to examine their own hearts on this subject. Our modern scientific society with its egocentric emphasis creates a formidable barrier to a correct understanding of the true gospel. We live in an age of rewards—an age of human glorification. Our proud, world-loving hearts clamor for recognition. Our educational system is built on the foundation of rewards. Our work force is rewarded on the basis of performance. Our pay scales, even church pay scales, are reward-oriented. The entire spectrum of sports is overwhelmingly related to rewards. The Olympic gold and silver awards are coveted almost above life itself! Some of the athletes in a recent Olympic competition were asked which they would choose—a gold medal with a shortened life, or a longer life without the medal. Some said they would accept an early death if they could only receive the gold medal!

The reward system is certainly found in Scripture, but it must never be confused with the gift of salvation by faith alone in Jesus Christ. Eternal life is a gift, not a reward. Salvation cannot be earned. It cannot be bought. It cannot be deserved even by the greatest Christian!

Finally, the enormous amount of energy and money spent on books and seminars designed to raise the level of self-esteem may give a sense of security to some. But nothing elevates a proper self-respect and appreciation for the value of one's own soul as much as an understanding of salvation by faith alone in the Lord Jesus Christ. When we behold the glory of the God of heaven and recognize to what depths our Saviour stooped to redeem us, we can then, and only then, begin to understand how valuable we really are. Such an understanding will eliminate any proud boasts of our achievements in the spiritual realm. One little ray of the glory of God, one gleam of the purity of Christ, one tiny vision of God's love exhibited on the cross makes it manifestly clear that attempts to work our way into heaven are based on a profound misunderstanding of the plan of salvation.

One wonders how many Christians of any persuasion have really grasped this tremendous truth.

Chapter 8

The Three Angels of Revelation

The book of Revelation—especially the symbolism of the beast, his image, and his mark—has puzzled Bible students for centuries, and from a human viewpoint it is easy to sympathize with those who feel that Revelation is difficult or impossible to understand, since much of it is written in symbolic language.

Yet the introductory verses announce that Revelation is a *revelation* of Jesus Christ, not an incomprehensible puzzle. Furthermore, a blessing is promised those who read, hear, and keep those things found in this prophetic book (1:1, 3). A similar blessing appears also in its climactic closing chapter: "Behold, I come quickly: blessed is he that keepeth the sayings of the prophecy of this book" (22:7). In order for us to be blessed because we read, hear, and keep the sayings of the prophecies of "this book," we obviously must have an understanding of what we read, hear, and keep. Surely it is not presumptuous to believe that the prophecies and messages between the opening and closing blessings are understandable under the direction and aid of the Holy Spirit.

Even in connection with the puzzling beast symbolism, chapter 15:2-3 declares that those who gain "the victory over the beast, and over his image, and over his mark, and over the number of his name" stand on the sea of glass singing the song of Moses and the song of the Lamb. It's a bit difficult to imagine such a group who have gotten victory over the beast and all that goes with it, and who even sing about it, are totally ignorant of the meaning of it all!

It is also rather curious that John, in his closing testimony, gives a severe warning against anyone who would add to or take away from the prophecies of this book. It almost seems as if, looking down through the future's halls, he anticipated those who would claim that Revelation is mysterious and incomprehensible. Such an attitude, it seems to me, takes away from the great truths God has in this book for the church in these latter days.

Finally, John closes Revelation with the thought that our Lord, the One who is the central theme of the book, has here given His testimony (22:20). Surely His witness and His testimony are not only true and reliable, but comprehensible.

The awe of Revelation 14:9-12

Bible students who agree that Revelation's prophecies contain important information that the church today can interpret and understand under the guidance of the Holy Spirit are nevertheless awed by chapter 14:9-12 because of the severity of its language. It is perhaps the most fearful denunciation to be found in Scripture, and this fact itself is a good reason to believe that we can understand its meaning. Would a God of infinite love give a warning message of such awful magnitude and such terrifying consequences if His servants are incapable of understanding its meaning? He would never require His people to avoid worship of the beast, nor threaten dire punishment for failure to obey, knowing they could never understand the symbols sufficiently to be obedient. It may be added that the tremendously negative aspects of this passage imply the existence of an equally tremendous positive truth. Counterfeit $20 notes are proofs of the existence of the genuine; no one produces counterfeit four-dollar notes! And the more marvelous the right way is, the more awful is the wrong.

It is true the warning is couched in somewhat mysterious terms. But before we dismiss it, we should recall that Noah's warning of a coming flood undoubtedly was labeled mysterious by the vast majority of his hearers. For a man to preach a world catastrophe in the form of a devastating flood seemed not only mysterious but ridiculous in those stormless, rain-free years. Attitudes toward Noah's warning probably differed little from current attitudes toward attempts to decipher and preach the meaning of Revelation 14:9-12 for today. Could this be one reason why Jesus declared, "As the days of Noe were, so shall also the coming of the Son of man be" (Matt. 24:37)?

To ignore the warning of Revelation 14:9-12 places one in a dangerous position. For whatever the beast power may represent, Revelation is convincingly clear regarding its scope, influence, and final disposition. Let's notice certain characteristics and descriptions of this power.

The beast power

We have already mentioned John's picture of a victorious group, standing on what appears to him as a sea of glass, singing the song of Moses and the song of the Lamb (see chap. 15:2, 3). These are identified as those who have gained the victory over the beast, his image, his mark, and the number of his name. The importance of this victory includes even more than ultimate deliverance from sin and death. In chapter 16:2, John explains that the first of the seven last plagues just prior to Christ's return falls on those who have the mark of the beast and who worship his image. The ultimate destruction of this power is described in chapters 19:20 and 20:10.

Chapter 13 contains the most detailed information about the beast. Those who worship this power ask rhetorical questions that indicate its strong influence and hold on the human race: "Who is like unto the beast? Who is able to make war with him?" (13:4). The picture of the beast drawn in this chapter is one of a power whose major characteristic is blasphemy against God, His name, His tabernacle, and those who dwell in heaven (13:6). Its power and influence extends over "all kindreds, and tongues, and nations" (13:7). And "all that dwell upon the earth shall worship him, whose names are not written in the book of life of the Lamb slain from the foundation of the world" (13:8).

A second beast is introduced in chapter 13 that makes an image to the first beast and causes "that as many as would not worship the image of the beast should be killed. And he causeth all, both small and great, rich and poor, free and bond, to receive a mark in their right hand, or in their foreheads" (13:15-16). Thus the beast, its image, and mark have worldwide, all-inclusive, all-powerful influence. It is against the force and influence of this powerful system that the Lord of the universe warns the human race in chapter 14:9-12.

The setting of Revelation 14:9-12

In considering this passage, we must take into account its setting. In the first five verses of chapter 14, John sees in vision a specific group of people known as the 144,000 who are "redeemed from the earth" (14:3). Although most commentators feel this number is symbolic, the important feature about this group is not their number but their unique spiritual experience, which includes (1) the "Father's name written in their foreheads," constituting the seal of God (14:1; see also 7:2-4); (2) a "new song" that they will sing "before the throne," for they have gone through a unique experience (14:3); (3) a total surrender to God, symbolized as undefiled virginity and seen in their practice of God's truth unmixed with error and tradition (14:4); (4) following the Lamb (Christ) wherever He goes, signifying total dependence, surrender, and obedience to Him (14:4); (5) guileless mouths, indicating a tremendous depth of Christian experience (14:5; see also James 3:2); and (6) standing "without fault before the throne of God," representing their trust in the righteousness of Christ rather than their own merits and works (14:5).

This faithful obedient group stands in stark contrast to those who "worship the beast and his image, and receive his mark in his forehead, or in his hand" (14:9). Obviously, this scene takes place *after* our Lord returns at the end of the age, or the end of the world history. But verses 6-12 of this same chapter set before us a description of a message that must go to the world *prior* to our Lord's return. It is a threefold preparatory message given to the world under the symbolism of three angels. The depth and scope of these messages have great significance, especially in view of developments that are taking place in these latter days. All three messages are inseparably woven together and cannot be fully understood unless studied as a whole. In other words, the third angel's message containing the warning against worshiping the beast has a direct connection with the first and second angels' messages.

The three angels

The first angel's message (14:6, 7) is a combined command and announcement of the "everlasting gospel" being preached to "every nation, and kindred, and tongue, and people." It is vital to keep in mind that the concept of "the everlasting gospel" being preached throughout all the earth is an introductory preface to all three messages. Actually, it is not merely an introductory remark but the theme, or core, or all three messages. This key point plays an important role in deciphering the symbolism of the mark of the beast. In opposition to the principles of "the everlasting gospel" stands a religious system that sweeps the world with a false gospel deceiving all except those whose names are written in the Lamb's book of life.

The second element in the first angel's message is the startling announcement that the hour of God's judgment is come (14:7). Then follows the command to fear God and worship Him as the creator of "heaven, earth, sea, and the fountains of water" (verse 7). This point is also of utmost significance, as we will see.

The second angel's message declares that "Babylon is fallen, . . . that great city, because she made all nations drink of the wine of the wrath of her fornication" (verse 8). Compare this verse carefully with John's vision of the great whore in chapter 17, "with whom the kings of the earth have committed fornication" (17:2). Also note that on this whore's forehead "was a name written, *mystery, Babylon the great, the mother of harlots and abominations of the earth*" (17:5). Obviously, John was not referring to the ancient city of Babylon, for it lay abandoned in ruins when he wrote these words, and continues to be so until this day. We can conclude only that the terminology is used symbolically to refer to the opponents of God's people, just as ancient Babylon was the unparalleled enemy of God's Old Testament people. "The wine of the wrath of her fornication" would represent the intoxicating sway she exercises over all who yield to her charms.

Following the second angel's message comes the third angel with his awful denunciation against those who "worship the beast and his image, and receive his mark in his forehead, or in his hand" (14:9).

The everlasting gospel

"The everlasting gospel" is the key to the symbolism of Revelation 14:9-12, especially that of the fall of Babylon and the mark of the beast. The grand, introductory theme of the first angel's message is the preaching of "the everlasting gospel" to earth dwellers of "every nation, tribe, language and people" (14:6, NIV). This "everlasting gospel" is thus basic to all that follows in this passage.

Some may wonder what is so unique or startling about the "everlasting gospel" to warrant the position of cruciality that is given these end-time messages. The answer lies not so much in the nature of the gospel itself. Indeed, the fact that it is the *everlasting* gospel indicates that it is the same gospel that was delivered to Adam, Enoch, Noah, Abraham, Daniel, the New Testament apostles, and that has been preserved intact through the vicissitudes of the church history to the present. The uniqueness of the gospel in this setting lies in its relationship to the succeeding messages of the second and third angels who accompany the first.

The announcements and warnings found in the second and third angels' messages must be seen in the context of right versus wrong, of the true (everlasting) gospel as opposed to a false gospel or gospels. In vivid contrast to the principles of the "everlasting gospel," a religious system undoubtedly composed of "every wind of doctrine" (Eph. 4:14) is brought to view, which defies not only the loyal subjects of Christ's spiritual kingdom but God Himself! For that reason it is proclaimed to be in a fallen condition, and dire warnings are issued against submitting oneself to it either voluntarily through deception or involuntarily through fear. With almost painful clarity, Rev. 14:12 draws this distinction between the genuine and the false—between those who retain the living principles of the "everlasting gospel" and those who clutch to their bosoms the false counterfeit. Yet, amazingly, this rebellious system sweeps the world with its false gospel, deceiving all except those whose names are written in the Lamb's book of life (Rev. 13:13-18; 17:8).

God has not overreacted to this challenge against His gospel. He directs the third angel to deliver denunciations unequaled for severity against the beast and his worshipers precisely because the nature of the false gospel so insidiously attempts to negate all that He has intended to accomplish (and *will* accomplish) through His "everlasting gospel." It is significant that the word John uses 36 times in chapters 13, 17, 19, and 20 to denote the "beast" is *therion*, meaning a dangerous, wild, ever venomous, beast. His choice of words leaves no doubt of the malignantly evil, malicious nature of this power.

When Adam sinned and came under the curse of death, all heaven was filled with the deepest sorrow. Then God's most precious gift, Jesus, was given for our salvation. The result? Profound rejoicing when a lost sheep is found. Universal praise throughout all heaven when a single sinner is saved (see Luke 15:3-7).

The incarnation, the cross, the Resurrection, the Second Coming, are the grand focal points of Scripture, and beautifully declare that nothing is of greater importance than our redemption. This is the theme, the gospel, of Scripture. Although proclaimed in a thousand ways through prophecy and parable, the point is that nothing can excel, or even equal, the "everlasting gospel." For that reason, nothing could be more execrable than a perversion of that gospel. What could equal in danger and deceptive terribleness a false plan of salvation that results not in salvation but in damnation? Jesus asked, "What good is it for a man to gain the whole world, yet forfeit his soul?" (Mark 8:36, NIV).

When Pilate examined our Lord in regard to His kingship and work as the Saviour of the race, He stated, "In fact, for this reason I was born, and for this I came into the world, to testify to the truth" (John 18:37, NIV). Christ came, lived, died, and was resurrected for the express purpose of seeking and saving "that which was lost" (Luke 19:10).

When we contemplate the mystery of redemption—the unbelievable love of God for a rebellious world—we must kneel before the Father and exclaim with Paul, Who can "grasp how wide and long and high and deep is the love of Christ, and to know this love that surpasses knowledge" (Eph. 3:18, 19, NIV). "God was in Christ reconciling the world unto himself" (2 Cor. 5:19). From beginning to end, the "everlasting gospel" is the core, the theme, the foundation, of Scripture. It is the focal point of heaven, and it should receive the constant attention of all humankind, especially the clergy. Our business and joy is to know the true gospel, to have a deep relationship with our Lord, and to communicate this glorious truth in the most loving and persuasive manner possible.

Irreconcilable conflict

Whatever precise identification one gives to the beast and his mark, it must ever be remembered that the basic concept is the irreconcilable conflict between the truth of the "everlasting gospel" on the one hand and the deceptive cunning of the beast on the other hand—a beast who is followed and worshiped by a majority of earth's multitudes. Both the issue and its results are delineated in Revelation 13 and 14. Those who, in loyalty to the Creator, refuse to worship and follow the beast and all that goes with it, will endure human wrath (chap. 13:8, 12, 15, 16). Those who yield allegiance to the beast and all that goes with it will endure the wrath of God (chap. 14:10).

Astonishingly, the controversy centers over the understanding or misunderstanding of the gospel. Thus is emphasized the need for the first angel's proclamation of the "everlasting gospel" to all the inhabitants of earth. Thus is also emphasized the necessity of having a clear understanding of the gospel. Yet how many, even among Christians, clearly understand this all-important subject?

One may wonder how it is possible for persecution, penalties, and death decrees to be heaped upon those who accept the "everlasting gospel." Yet this should not be too surprising. Since the plan of salvation was put into effect, such opposition has been the case, although never on such a worldwide scale or with such intensity as is brought to view in Revelation 14:6-12.

The great controversy

The reality of Satan is expressly taught in Scripture. Jesus Himself not only knew the authenticity of Satan, but constantly felt the effects of the great conflict raging between Himself and Satan over His plan to save men and women. If the gospel plan runs like a golden thread from Genesis to Revelation and constitutes the ultimate theme of Scripture, then what must be the battle plan of Satan? The answer is obvious! It is to destroy, wreck, pervert, oppose, downgrade, and make of none effect God's gospel with every artifice at this command. This is the great purpose of the enemy and his cohorts.

This conflict between Christ and Satan, between the true and the false gospel, can be seen at the gates of Eden itself in the antagonism of Cain toward Abel. Both were the sons of Adam. Both were sinners. Both were acquainted with the plan of salvation, as illustrated in the system of sacrificial offerings. Both knew that without the shedding of blood there was no remission of sins. Both acknowledged God's claim for reverence and worship. Both knew that the sacrificial system typified the coming of the Redeemer. Both erected altars. Both brought an offering. But now comes the difference, and it is a vast one! Cain followed his own wishes by bringing a bloodless offering, the fruits of his own labor. But Abel, in submissive obedience, by faith "offered unto God a more excellent sacrifice than Cain" (Heb. 11:4). Note carefully that the wrath of Cain, symbolic of the world's wrath upon those who follow Jesus fully and explicitly in these last days, was directed toward his brother, and his jealousy, which turned into hatred, found fruitage in murder. He murdered Abel not for any wrong Abel had done but "because his own actions were evil and his brother's were righteous" (1 John 3:12, NIV). How true it is that "everyone who does evil hates the light, and will not come into the light for fear that his deeds will be exposed" (John 3:20, NIV).

The seal and mark principle

Here, very early in Scripture, one sees what may be called the "mark of the beast" principle, as opposed to the "seal of God" principle. In Revelation 7, John speaks of the servants of God who are sealed by Him, as opposed to those described in chapters 13 and 14 who are marked by the beast as a symbol of their allegiance to his system. Although this mark and seal principle may be traced throughout Scripture, there are unique, identifiable elements in the seal and mark that have fulfillment only in these last days. The same opposing principles underlying the seal and mark that are to be found throughout sacred history are brought to their universal and ultimate struggle and resolution in these verses. Indeed, despite the fearful excoriation of the beast, his worshipers, and their false gospel, the entire passage carries a triumphant ring. Every word seems to breathe ultimate victory over the enemies of God and His truth.

The context of this passage show that from a chronological viewpoint these messages are designed for the last days, both to confront every individual on earth with the inescapable responsibility to decide for or against God's everlasting gospel, and also to prepare and enable those who choose God to stand with heaven in spite of almost overwhelming pressure from the worshipers and followers of the beast. John gives these messages their proper place in prophetic history when in the verse following them he relates that he saw "a white cloud, and upon the cloud one sat like unto the Son of man, having on his head a golden crown, and in his hand a sharp sickle" (Rev. 14:14).

As we stated, although the principle of the mark and seal may be traced throughout Scripture, there are unique, identifiable elements in both, which have fulfillment only in these last days. The seal of God and Satan's opposing mark are brought to their final, universal struggle and resolution in the verses constituting the three angels' messages of Revelation 14.

Daniel 7 and Revelation 13

Daniel 7 throws light on the symbolism of the beast found in Revelation 13. In Daniel 7 we find world history clearly symbolized by a lion, leopard, bear, and a horrendous, indescribable fourth beast. The identification of Daniel's beast symbols is not left to speculation. Daniel 7:17 specifically states that the four beasts represent four kings (or kingdoms, according to the LXX, Theodotian, and the Vulgate). Daniel 7:23 equates the fourth beast with the fourth kingdom. Most scholars agree that the four beasts of Daniel 7 represent the same world empires symbolized by the image of gold, silver, brass, iron, and clay of Daniel 2.

Beginning with the Babylonian Empire, symbolized by the head of gold in Daniel 2 and by the lion in Daniel 7, we can easily trace the identity of the other symbols as verified by history.

Coming to Revelation 13:1, 2, we find the beast depicted there to be a composite of the four beasts found in Daniel 7. John alludes to these characteristics in the reverse order of their appearance in Daniel, since he starts with the world government at the time of his writing, Rome, and then traces the line back to Babylon.

We should note also that the beast with its mark that God warns against in Revelation 14:9-12 is undoubtedly the same as the beast of Revelation 13:1, 2. Revelation 14 specifically refers to the beast and his image, while Revelation 13 describes this beast and the creation of an image to it. The beast and its image are united in their demands that men and women receive the mark of the beast. Thus anyone who worships the beast also worships the image and is a bearer of the mark.

The role of the antichrist

In our study of the beast and its mark, we need to keep in mind that the story of Revelation is the story of Christ versus antichrist. Especially in chapters 11 to 20 do we find antichrist occupying the scene. Next to Christ Himself, antichrist is the most prominent feature of the book. The actual word *antichrist* is not found in Revelation, but the meaning is. It is a term that clearly refers to one who is opposed to Christ, against Christ, instead of Christ. All these rebellious roles assume the prerogatives of Christ and militate not only against His person but also against His spirit and principles. The term *antichrist* appears in the New Testament only in the writings of John (1 John 2:18, 22; 4:3; 2 John 7). In these passages the apostle assumes his readers' knowledge concerning antichrist and that they believe the antichrist's full manifestation will be in connection with the last days.

As a result, John does not specifically identify antichrist as a particular person or organization. So also the beast symbolism in Revelation 13 and 14 far transcends any identification of a specific individual, emperor, or other personage. Rather it is a composite power. Paul describes the same power in 2 Thessalonians 2:7-12 as a developing apostasy, beginning in the days of the apostles and culminating in the manifestation of the "man of sin" or "man of lawlessness," who opposes God by sitting in the temple of God and equating himself with God. Furthermore the work of this spiritual kingdom of evil climaxes with the Second Coming of Jesus Christ, who will destroy the antichrist, the beast, the dragon, the scarlet-clad woman, and all those associated with them.

It should also be noted that the dragon of Revelation 12, specifically identified as Satan, is the one who gives the beast his power, seat, and authority (see Rev. 13:2). Thus there is an unholy confederacy of evil that permeates earthly powers and kingdoms manifested throughout history. It is an unholy union of political and religious power, which seeks to dominate and control the minds of men not only through force but by means of intrigue, falsehood, and error.

The controversy theme is continued in the two women of Revelation 12 and 17, embracing the faithful and the faithless of all ages. In Revelation 17 we see what some interpret as a symbol of an apostate church—a woman riding on a scarlet-colored beast, full of blasphemous names, with seven heads and ten horns. This gaudily clad woman is in marked contrast to the sun-clothed woman representing true Christianity in Revelation 12. The apostate woman is arrayed in purple and scarlet, bedecked with gold and jewels and pearls, holding in her hand a golden cup full of abominations and the impurities of her fornication, and on her forehead is written the name of "mystery: Babylon the great, mother of harlots and of earth's abominations" (see Rev. 17:4, 5, RSV). Many Bible students have identified this woman, drunk with the blood of saints, as Rome in both its phases of pagan and spiritual apostasy. The apostle Paul saw this spiritual apostasy working within the church very early (see Acts 20:29, 30). The persecutions and martyrdom of pagan Rome were few compared with those in later centuries.

It is not our purpose to indict any now living, whatever their spiritual heritage. All who oppose Christ and His church, either by persecuting cruelty or doctrinal counterfeit, come under the heading of antichrist. Above all, Satan himself, as Revelation 12 portrays him, is the supreme antichrist. Yet he rarely works against Christ in a direct, open confrontation, but through individuals and religious and political institutions.

Varied meanings of beast

Thus the beast has repeated application. First to pagan Rome; second, to the medieval persecutions of the state church; and last, in the final days of earth's history to a revival of a political and religious persecuting power that seeks to destroy Christ's faithful, patient remnant.

The climax of Revelation 13, combined with the third angel's message of Revelation 14 describing God's warning against those who receive the mark of the beast, clearly indicates a worldwide enforcement of a "mark" under pain of boycott and death. The Greek word for "mark" is *charagma*, which means an etching, a stamp, a badge of servitude, or a sculptured figure. Note carefully that the image to the beast figures prominently in Revelation 13. This symbolism draws heavily from Daniel 3, where a death decree initiated by Babylon is connected with the worship of an image. In essence John is saying that the same situation found in ancient Babylon (in which a political-religious power demanded worship on pain of death) will prevail on a worldwide basis in the last days.

The climax of the third angel's message with its warning against worshiping the beast and receiving his mark is found in Revelation 14, verse 12: "Here is a call for the endurance of the saints, for those who keep the commandments of God and the faith of Jesus" (RSV). Central in the controversy between Christ and

Satan is the relationship of law and grace, which is so greatly misunderstood by many today. Organized religion seems to fluctuate between the equally fatal extremes of antinomianism and legalism.

In connection with this concept, it is significant to note that God's faithful followers—those who are protected by His seal instead of receiving the mark of the beast—are described as commandment keepers (Rev. 14:12). The worshipers of the beast, in contrast, violate the first commandment, for they worship the beast (chap. 13:8); the second commandment, for they worship an image of the beast (verse 15); the third commandment, for they prefer the name of the beast to the name of the Creator (verse 17); and the fourth commandment, for no idolater can rightly observe the memorial of Him who created all things.

The fourth commandment, which calls men to remember the Sabbath day to keep it holy on the basis of God's Creatorship, is echoed in the first angel's message of Revelation 14:6, 7, which commands every nation, kindred, tongue, and people to worship God who made "heaven, and earth, and the sea, and the fountains of waters." What an appropriate command in these last hours of earth's history, when the inroads of evolutionary concepts have to a large extent obliterated from the minds of earth's inhabitants the creative power and acts of the God of the universe. These are memorialized by the fourth commandment. Those disloyal to their Creator and Redeemer find it impossible to experience true worship.

When Babylon's King Nebuchadnezzar recovered from the beast syndrome (see Daniel 4), the record says that he lifted his eyes to heaven and his own testimony states that "my reason returned to me, and I blessed the Most High, and praised and honored him who lives for ever" (Dan. 4:34, RSV). When will men know and understand that God is supreme, God is the Creator, God rules the universe? Beasts look down to the earth, not up to their Creator in praise and acknowledgement. Not until Nebuchadnezzar lifted his eyes to Heaven was his reason restored. This is an important point. Nebuchadnezzar's disgraceful downfall to be a subject of the beast kingdom was a result of his own self-glorification and pride of achievement. "Is not this great Babylon, which I have built by my mighty power and as a royal residence and for the glory of my majesty?" (verse 30, RSV). The record states that while the words were still in his mouth his kingdom was taken from him and he became like an animal. The same self-magnification is the basic principle also of those who worship the beast and receive his mark. The line is thus drawn between those who acknowledge that they are but creatures and worship their Maker in harmony with His prescribed way and those who worship the creature—themselves and others like themselves—and worship not in the way God prescribes but in their own way.

Thus John paints the issue as obedience or disobedience to God's commandments. The test in the last days will not center primarily on the commandments of the second table of the law—our relationship to others—but on the first four, which deal with our relationship to God. All unrighteousness grows out of ungodliness. We cannot behave properly toward our fellow humans if we are not in a right relationship to God (see Rom. 1:18). Thus the test centers on the first table, not the second. And the first table of the law revolves around the recognition of God as Creator. In fact, the whole plan of salvation has as its basic underpinning the doctrine of Creation. Think it not strange that throughout all Scripture prominence is given to the Creation doctrine. Carl H. F. Henry says, "The doctrine of creation is so basic as to be the indispensable foundation for any tolerable, viable human existence. The proof of this is being spelled out in the progressive disintegration of the spirit and life of modern, homeless man. When the truth of this is clearly seen, the Church will speak about God the Father, Almighty, maker of heaven and earth, with a new relevance to today's growing crowd of lonely men, to its lost and nameless, to its homeless and hopeless men."[1]

Antichrist as a system

We have seen so far that the concept of antichrist, portrayed by various symbols in the books of both Daniel and Revelation, is not merely some past, present, or future personage but rather a system that deceives and destroys God's truth and people. Of course, systems and organizations do not exist apart from individuals. Nazism, for example, cannot be separated from Hitler. And just as Hitler and his system collapsed after a short, horrible period, so, too, will the beast-antichrist confederacy collapse when the great controversy between Christ and Satan culminates in victory for Christ at His Second Coming.

Blasphemy—contempt for God, His character, His will, His laws—is a major hallmark of this system (see Rev. 13:1, 5, 6). This contempt for God and all He represents is characterized by the worship not of the true God but of the human-made beast system. One of the parallels between the beast system and God's last message for earth (symbolized by the three angels' messages) is that both require worship. In fact, Revelation 12-14 describes the final struggle between Christ and Satan being over this feature of worship. We are created to worship God, and even fallen human beings will worship some thing, system, or person.

The two camps

Thus the world will be divided into two camps—those who worship the beast, or antichrist, system and those who worship the Creator God.

In light of these thoughts, note that the blasphemous antichrist system so vividly described in Revelation 13:1-10 is not necessarily an avowed atheistic power. Atheism, by its very nature, is part of this worldwide system opposed to God, but the worst blasphemy is not that of an atheist who shakes his fist in God's face. Far more reprehensible and insidious (and therefore more dangerous) are professing Christians who, despite their outward appearance, are strangers to the actual character of Christ and allow themselves to be used as Satan's agent within the church itself. The rebuke of Christ to the Laodicean church (Rev. 3:14-22), which is symbolic of the condition of His followers in these last days, is significant: "I know thy works, that thou art neither cold nor hot: I would thou wert cold or hot. So then because thou art lukewarm, and neither cold nor hot, I will spue thee out of my mouth" (3:15, 16).

The open rebellion of the avowed non-Christians is a far less threat to Christ and His church than the lukewarm professed Christians who worship God only on their own terms. Thus the word *lukewarm* describes far more than sitting in the pew only at Easter and Christmas accompanied by spasmodic financial support. Lukewarmness includes failure to ascertain God's will through careless-ness in serious study of the Scriptures; parroting of error because the majority would have it so; loyalty to a religious system merely because of family tradition; rationalizing disobedience to specific commands of God for the sake of unity and peace; acceptance of false principles in order to satisfy self-indulgent desires; and attempting to control minds through illicit use of religion. Numerous illustrations of these and other blasphemous characteristics of lukewarmness are to be found in history and current events. The point is that blasphemy in one of its ugliest forms rears its head within the church itself in the person of those who claim God's name but reject His authority over their lives. These may appear to be worshipers of God, but in essence they worship other gods.

Two homes, two foundations

Too often we preach on Jesus' parable (Matt. 7:21-23) of the home built on foundations of sand and forget the preamble as well as the point of the parable itself. The introduction reveals that not all professed Christians will enter the kingdom. The Saviour here is not speaking to atheists or to a non-Christian society, but to those who have prophesied, cast out devils, and performed many wonderful things—all in the name of Christ. Why is it that many of these will hear the words "depart from me, ye that work iniquity"? The answer is plain. They have failed to conform their lives to God's will and to operate on the principles of His kingdom. They have created their own religious system and labeled it Christianity. Revelation 14:12 indicates that obedience is the foundation of true worship. Anything less is iniquitous. What could be more blasphemous than a self-proclaimed Christian who is actually working at cross purposes to God? Such are "workers of iniquity."

Returning to the parable, we find two homes on two different foundations—sand and stone. Note that the common denominator is that both builders erect homes and both builders are aware of how to build safely and correctly. The vari-able is that one obediently built on the bedrock according to the instructions of the Master Designer while the other contemptuously, blasphemously, built on the flimsy sand. Here again we see the element of true worship versus false worship.

Obviously, the rock foundation represents Christ. Building on Him represents those who base their lives on Him. Connecting this parable with the prophet Isaiah's words gives a more complete picture: "Therefore thus saith the Lord God, Behold, I lay in Zion for a foundation a stone, a tried stone, a precious corner stone, a sure foundation: he that believeth shall not make haste" (Isa. 28:16).

Worship and loyalty

All true worship is based on loyalty to God's commands, and nothing can take the place of absolute obedience to His will. King Saul at Gilgal appeared to be quite conscientious as he stood before Israel's army and offered a sacrifice to God, but his piety was hypocritical (see 1 Sam. 15). The king of Israel performed a religious worship service in direct opposition to the explicit commands of God! This was not the first time Saul had set aside God's commands to follow the way that seemed right to him. Like many today, Saul was accustomed to making decisions on the basis of political, economic, or spiritual expediency rather than on the basis of strict fidelity to God. Thus God gave him his final opportunity to demonstrate his loyalty by commanding him to utterly destroy the Amalekites, including their livestock.

Despite God's careful instructions, presumption led Saul to follow his own inclination. On his way home from the most brilliant victory that he had ever gained, Saul met the prophet Samuel, who had been sent to him by God. Debased by his disobedience, Saul greeted Samuel with lying lips: "Blessed be thou of the Lord: I have performed the commandment of the Lord. And Samuel said, What meaneth then this bleating of the sheep in my ears, and the lowing of the oxen which I hear?" (1 Sam. 15:13, 14).

Saul began to excuse his disobedience by explaining that he had spared the best animals for sacrifices to God. When Samuel began to relate God's message of rebuke, Saul defiantly protested that he *had* done God's will. Samuel replied, "Hath the Lord as great delight in burnt offerings and sacrifices, as in obeying the voice of the Lord? Behold, to obey is better than sacrifice, and to hearken than the fat of rams. For rebellion is as the sin of witchcraft, and stubbornness is as iniquity and idolatry. Because thou hast rejected the word of the Lord, he hath also rejected thee from being king" (1 Sam. 15:22, 23).

This story perhaps best describes the issues at stake in the conflict between Satan and Christ as carried out by their followers—the beast worshipers of Revelation 13 and God's remnant of Revelation 14:12 "that keep the commandments of God, and the faith of Jesus." This latter group builds on Christ, the true foundation, not on some human-made sand foundation that cannot stand the test. Those who build on Him learn that worshiping the true God requires careful obedience to His building instructions.

It should be emphasized repeatedly that the only truly important thing in life is our eternal salvation. "What shall it profit a man, if he shall gain the whole world, and lose his own soul? Or what shall a man give in exchange for his soul?" (Mark 8:36, 37). The incomparable value of our salvation is best seen in the cost of the cross. In the light of the pricelessness of salvation, any attempt to change, ignore, or reject God's plan to save man is *blasphemy*. Any attempt to divert human minds from Christ to an organization, a theory, or a person is *blasphemy*.

Any substitution or counterfeit for the true gospel is *blasphemy*.

Thus, the Lord's ultimate concern for humanity is salvation—nothing more, nothing less, and nothing else. The ultimate concern of the prince of evil is to destroy humanity, and his most insidious way of destruction is to entice us with a counterfeit gospel. No wonder Jesus describes Satan as a murderer and such a liar that there is no truth in him (John 8:44; 10:10). The beast described in Revelation 13:2 receives his power, throne, and great authority from Satan the dragon (see Rev. 12:9), and thus has similar characteristics. It is this beast-antichrist conglomerate that is the object of the most fearful threatenings God ever addressed to mortals: "If any man worship the beast and his image, and receive his mark in his forehead, or in his hand, the same shall drink of the wine of the wrath of God, which is poured out without mixture into the cup of his indignation" (Rev. 14:9, 10). Only those whose names are in the Lamb's book of life will be spared (see Rev. 13:8).

What is the basic difference between those who worship the beast and his image and those who worship the Lamb, Christ Jesus? It is the same difference found between those who build on the Rock and those who build on the sand. The difference is two methods of salvation that can be traced from Genesis to Revelation. One is salvation by human methods and works, the other is salvation through grace by faith in Jesus Christ.

---

[1]   *Christianity Today*, Jan. 5, 1962, p. 3.

Chapter 9

Tithe is the Lord's

Covetousness, greed, and self-glorification constitute the sandy foundation on which the carnal-minded stand. These ever-present evils are common to both secular and Christian society. If for no other reason, God gave us stewardship to alleviate the plague of greed. Returning tithe to God testifies that we recognize we are His because of both creation and redemption. Tithing keeps the owner-manager concept fresh in our thinking.

Giving our tithes and offerings is God's major cure for greedy self-glorification. Our growth in sanctification is directly related to our giving. Consistently sharing our wealth for the fulfillment of the gospel commission is the secret of abundant living (see Isaiah 58; Daniel 4:27; Luke 12:33).

In the act of giving our tithe to God, there is a spiritual element that helps us sense that life and all of our possessions are sacred and that we must use them to God's honor and glory. The moment that we, personally or corporately, begin to handle tithe funds carelessly, we may breach barriers that stand to prevent us from getting involved in financial situations that are a dishonor to God's cause. For this reason I do not advocate individuals directing the use of their own tithe.

The methods that some leaders of independent ministries use in appealing for funds are deplorable. They circulate articles, letters, and books among the members of the church decrying the sins of the organization. This attack implies that their own programs are free of apostasy and error. Then some of these individuals suggest that since Ellen White at times used tithe at her discretion, their followers would be justified in sending their tithes to support their programs.

Undoubtedly these tactics siphon off tithe from God's storehouse to independent storehouses. If an independent ministry is accountable only to its leader or to boards that have little or no knowledge about its financial affairs, this opens the possibility of the serious misuse of funds.

Early Adventist tithe-use practices

What did our church in its early years understand about how the tithe was to be used? Apparently their understanding of the basis on which believers gave tithes and offerings and of the precise use of these funds underwent a gradual development. We can summarize by saying, though, that in our early years both tithes and offerings were channeled almost exclusively toward ministerial support.

The form of systematic benevolence first adopted by Sabbathkeeping Adventists (in 1859) consisted of the setting aside of a weekly offering of from 5 to 25 cents for men and from 2 to 10 cents for women. In 1864 this system expanded to include a weekly gift of 2 cents for each $100 worth of property each member possessed. It was not until the late 1870s that emphasis was placed on giving the tithe as a percentage of income.

Prior to 1880, the instruction we have from the Spirit of Prophecy does not delineate precisely how systematic benevolence was to be used—nor were restrictions imposed until later years. We do know, however, that in the church's infancy, neither the medical, the publishing, nor the educational branches of the work were regular recipients of tithe funds.

(However, Ellen White did write a testimony in 1879 in which referring to the erection of churches and the establishing of schools and publishing houses, she said: "These institutions are ordained of God and should be sustained by tithes and liberal offerings."[1] This testimony gives an overall view of God's require-ments in the area of stewardship. Giving was to far exceed the tithe. Ellen White refers to a "conscientious few" in Old Testament times who gave one third of all their income.)

In 1880, James White wrote, "A tithe is the Lord's. Since the Fall it has been necessary that there should be people devoted wholly to the service of God. It appears that from the very beginning the Lord taught His people to devote one tenth to the support of His ministers."[2]

An action taken at the General Conference session that same year indicates that some local churches were using tithe funds for church expense. The action reads, "Resolved, That no church should devote any portion of its tithe to the erection or repairing of its church, without the free consent of the state confer-ence committee."[3]

Butler liberalizes tithe policy

While the concept of the use of tithes was evolving, it was generally under-stood at this time that tithe funds were to be reserved for the gospel ministry. Shortly thereafter, this practice was liberalized. According to an undated pamphlet (possibly 1884), General Conference president G. I. Butler believed that the many demands facing the church legitimized using the tithe for auditors, tract and missionary state secretaries, colporteurs, and so forth. Butler acknowledged that in some cases the gospel ministry suffered because of a lack of funds, but concluded, "We believe the tithing is designed of God for the support, as far as it will go, of all laborers who are called by the cause of God to give their time to His work. We know of no other special system for this purpose."[4]

The extent to which Butler's opinions affected the working policies of the church is a matter of conjecture. However, in a special, separately published pamphlet, Ellen White later clarified the use of tithe: "The light which the Lord has given me on this subject is that the means in the treasury for the support of the ministers in the different fields is not to be used for any other purpose."[5]

She spoke against the practice of some church leaders in using the tithe for other expenses: to keep up the meetinghouse or for some charity. Instead, she urged that "house-to-house labor be done in setting before the families in Battle

Creek and Oakland their duty in acting apart in meeting these expenses, which may be called common or secular, and let not the treasury be robbed."[6]

Yet she allowed for exceptions: "There are exceptional cases, where poverty is so deep that in order to secure the humblest place of worship, it may be necessary to appropriate the tithes."[7]

The next year Ellen White unequivocally restated the concept that tithe is to be used for the gospel ministry: "God's ministers are His shepherds, appointed by Him to feed His flock. The tithe is His provision for their maintenance, and He designs that it shall be held sacred to this purpose."[8] Six years later she reaffirmed this clear position: "The tithe is to be used for one purpose—to sustain the ministers whom the Lord has appointed to do His work."[9] This counsel included both men and women. In 1899 she wrote, "The tithe should go to those who labor in word and doctrine, be they men or women."[10]

In statements that appeared in late 1900, she advocated using tithe for Bible teachers in our schools. She wrote, "Those who minister in our schools, teaching the Word of God, explaining the Scriptures, educating the students in the things of God, should be supported by the tithe money. This instruction was given long ago, and more recently it has been repeated again and again."[11]

Emphasizing the Bible teacher's role as a minister, she said, "The best ministerial talent should be employed in teaching the Bible in our schools. Those selected for this work need to be thorough Bible students and to have a deep Christian experience, and their salary should be paid from the tithe."[12]

As to the maintenance of church schools, she advocated, with qualifications, using a second tithe.[13] Finally, she wrote a very significant statement on the use of tithe in 1904, portions of which were to form a part of the counsels that eventually were published in *Testimonies* under the title "Faithful Stewardship." One paragraph reads, "One reasons that the tithe may be applied to school purposes. Still others reason that canvassers and colporteurs should be supported from the tithe. But a great mistake is made when the tithe is drawn from the object for which it is to be used—the support of the ministers. There should be today in the field 100 well-qualified laborers where now there is but one."[14]

Ellen White's use of tithe

How did Ellen White use the tithe? Those who use stories about her tithe practices to support the diversion of tithe from the conference treasury do her a disservice. Volume 5 of Arthur White's recent biography of Ellen White reveals that at times she handled tithe funds in a way that has perplexed some.[15] The evidence supports the conclusion that she was a careful and faithful tither. In 1890 she stated, "I pay my tithe gladly and freely, saying, as did David, 'Of thine own have we given thee.'"[16]

Those who are concerned that their tithe is being misused would do well to consider her remark, "Unworthy ministers may receive some of the means thus raised, but dare anyone, because of this, withhold from the treasury and brave the curse of God? I dare not."[17]

When she used tithe outside of the regular channels, she did so to help ministers who were going through experiences of want and suffering similar to what she and her husband had known in their early years. She stated, "And where I see workers in this cause that have been true and loyal to the work, who are left to suffer, it is my duty to speak in their behalf. If this does not move the brethren to help them, then I must help them, even if I am obliged to use a portion of my tithe in doing so."[18]

Her son, W. C. White, pointed out that many times the conferences responded to her requests and gave the needed help. But in some cases in which the conference was short of funds or the worker was not appreciated properly, she would say to her bookkeeper, "Send help as soon as you can, and if necessary take it from my tithe."[19]

Controversy over one such case moved Ellen White to write the following to the conference president involved: "It has been presented to me for years that my tithe was to be appropriated by myself to aid the white and colored ministers who were neglected and did not receive sufficient, properly to support their families. When my attention was called to aged ministers, white or black, it was my special duty to investigate into their necessities and supply their needs. This was to be my special work, and I have done this in a number of cases. No man should give notoriety to the fact that in special cases the tithe is used in that way. . . .

"I have been instructed to do this; and as the money is not withheld from the Lord's treasury, it is not a matter that should be commented upon, for it will necessitate my making known these matters, which I do not desire to do, because it is not best."[20] She ended the letter by saying, "Circumstances alter cases. I would not advise that anyone should make a practice of gathering up tithe money. But for years there have now and then been persons who have lost confidence in the appropriation of the tithe who have placed their tithe in my hands, and said that if I did not take it they would themselves appropriate it to the families of the most needy ministers they could find. I have taken the money, given a receipt for it, and told them how it was appropriated.

"I write this to you so that you shall keep cool and not become stirred up and give publicity to this matter, lest many more shall follow their example."[21]

Note carefully that the money was always used for the support of the ministers. Ellen White used all tithe funds she handled for the purposes for which tithe was intended to be used. In addition, none today have had direct instruction from the Lord to gather tithe for themselves or their independent ministries or to direct their tithe outside of church channels.

Ellen White's use of the tithe does not justify our using the tithe according to our own whims or desires. If every member of the church did so, our world organization would crumble and our mission would suffer greatly. In 1911 another brother in the church wrote to Ellen White asking if he could send his tithe for her to handle. She replied, "You ask if I will accept tithe from you and use it in the cause of God where most needed. In reply I will say that I shall not refuse to do this, but at the same time I will tell you that there is a better way.

"It is better to put confidence in the ministers of the conference where you live, and in the officers of the church where you worship. Draw nigh to your brethren. Love them with a true heart fervently, and encourage them to bear their responsibilities faithfully in the fear of God. 'Be thou an example of the believers, in word, in conversation, in charity, in spirit, in faith, in purity.'"[22]

The tithe is the Lord's

Scripture is clear that the tithe is the Lord's, not ours. We get it to Him by bringing it to His storehouse, the church, even as God's people did in Nehemiah's and Hezekiah's day (see Nehemiah 10; 2 Chronicles 31). The equivalent for the word *storehouse* in Malachi 3:10 is *treasury*. In both Old and New Testaments it is clear that the treasury for the tithe is the house of the Lord, not a private foundation or even an independent ministry, regardless of how good it may be. The issue is ecclesiological in nature. Either we believe that God has an organized church on earth and it is our duty and privilege to bring the tithe into the treasury of the church, or we virtually set up our own church and direct the use of our tithe.

Leadership, in turn, has a responsibility before God to use these funds properly. We must be accountable to both God and our constituency. Furthermore, we have the responsibility of giving our own tithe to God through church channels and teaching our members to do likewise.

It is my firm belief that this is God's church, and as long as I am a member of this body, I have no right to withhold or divert my tithe at my discretion.

---

1   *Testimonies*, vol. 4, p. 464.
2   "Tithes and Offerings," *Review and Herald*, Jan. 15, 1880, p. 35.
3   *Review and Herald*, Oct. 14, 1880, p. 252.
4   G. I. Butler, *An Examination of the Tithing System From a Bible Standpoint* (Battle Creek, Mich: Review and Herald, c. 1884), p. 72.
5   *Special Testimonies to Ministers and Workers*, Series A, No. 10 (n.p., n.s. [1897]), p. 18.
6   *Ibid.*, p. 19.
7   Manuscript 24, 1897.
8   Manuscript 139, 1898.
9   Manuscript 82, 1904.
10   *Evangelism*, p. 492.
11   *Testimonies*, vol. 6, p. 215.
12   *Ibid.*, pp. 134, 135.
13   Manuscript 67, 1901; see also letter 167, 1904.
14   *Testimonies*, vol. 9, pp. 248, 249.

15   See Arthur White, *Ellen G. White: The Early Elmshaven Years* (Washington, D.C.: Review and Herald Pub. Assn., 1981), pages 392-397.
16   *Ibid.*, p. 392.
17   *Ibid.*
18   *Ibid.*, p. 393.
19   *Ibid.*, p. 393, quoting a letter by W. C. White.
20   *Ibid.*, p. 395.
21   *Ibid.*, pp. 395, 396.
22   *Ibid.*, p. 397.

Chapter 10

The Uniqueness of Adventism

Seventh-day Adventists have always seen themselves as a divinely called movement charged with restoring a comprehensive system of truth to the world prior to the return of Christ as Lord. Is this exclusivism?

Is the Seventh-day Adventist Church the "Noah's ark," the only "fold of safety" in modern times? Are we being exclusivists or narrow-minded for thinking so? Are our doctrines true and free from error in the broad themes they set forth? Do we have additional truths, or perspective of truth, not found in other religious organizations? If not, what right do we have to invite those of a different religious persuasion to unite with us?

There are some who want to separate "beliefs" from Christ and our experience with Him. But Christ, His deity and Lordship, His atoning sacrifice and all that goes with it, must *be believed* before He can become a spiritual experience in our hearts. If we believe in the reality of a "great controversy" in which "we wrestle not against flesh and blood, but against principalities, against powers" (Eph. 6:12), a system of beliefs, doctrines if you please, must be at the center. All that Scripture teaches can be summed up in a set of doctrines or beliefs, and it is this that gives focus and content to our spiritual experience.

Therefore the prince of darkness, well acquainted with Scripture, works perseveringly and malignantly to deceive the very elect, not only by twisting Scripture but by destroying confidence in its authority. Thus he has magnificently confused the human race and spawned a multiplicity of concepts not in harmony with a plain "Thus saith the Lord."

Restoration of truth

On the other hand, God heroically attempts, through individuals and groups, to bring the world back into the pathway of truth. It is important to note in this great controversy view that whenever reformations have occurred and God's truth has beamed brightly upon the world, that which comes to light is not so much the newness or uniqueness of the truth but rather a rediscovery of truths that have been given to the world from the very beginning. In reference to our own movement we should understand that our uniqueness must not depend upon or be equated with the originality of a particular truth. Rather it is based on a restoration of truth. Through this movement, truth long buried under tradition and philosophy has been brought back into focus. If the eyeglasses through which we discern truth become opaque through error and superstition, the cleaning of the glasses does not make the truth unique or new; it simply restores it to its original clarity. God's truth, as revealed in His Word, has been made of none effect through centuries of both neglect and opposition, but now it is being brought back to a condition of clarity, brilliance, and effectiveness in the life.

Isaiah speaks of those who "shall build the old waste places" and calls them "the repairer of the breach, the restorer of paths to dwell in" (Isa. 58:12). The Jews' moral edifice lay in ruins, and a great work of rebuilding through revival, reformation, and restoration was needed. A breach in the wall, resulting from failure to practice true religion, needed repairing. Verse 13 refers to the restoration of true Sabbathkeeping. This is a very significant passage for our church today when the three angels' messages of Revelation 14 includes the restoration of the Sabbath to its rightful place in the lives of men and women.

The long line of restorers

In our role as "repairers of the breach, restorers of paths to dwell in," we simply stand at the end of a long line of those who have done a similar work from the beginning of truth's perversion by sin. Biblical history indicates numerous victories and failures for God's truth. When Adam and Eve sinned, they lost not only their perfect spiritual nature but their face-to-face fellowship with God. Their concepts of Him and His truth inevitably began to deteriorate rapidly, influenced by a "fig-leaf theology." God did everything possible to help them understand that there was only one way, one plan, one truth to follow. Satan so despised this singleness of God's way, its exclusiveness and uniqueness, that he inspired the first murder over it. Cain felt there must be at least two ways, but God said only one. This initial experience is but a microcosm of all human history since.

Noah and his family are another outstanding example of the unique and exclusive nature of restored truth. Noah's preaching was totally out of harmony with the theological and scientific thinking of his day. His core message of salvation by faith alone in the Lord is identical in its essentials to the core message of our church today—the everlasting gospel. He preached in the setting of a world to be destroyed by water; we preach in the setting of a coming world destruction by fire.

Likewise, in God's call to Abraham we see a most intriguing aspect of exclusiveness. Because Abraham and his family clung to a knowledge of the true God in the midst of superstition and heathenism, God chose him and his descendants to serve as His handpicked representatives in preserving and restoring His truth. A man who was willing to sacrifice his only son surely had special insight into God's love shown through the sacrifice of His only begotten Son, but did Abraham's teaching and example to the heathen tribes about him produce any new truth? Never! What he believed and practiced was as old as Adam and Eve. Because of his faithfulness he was promised, "In thee shall all families of the earth be blessed" (Gen. 12:3).

Moses, too, son of slave parents, had the finger of God placed upon him. A slave leading slaves! Truly God has chosen the foolish things of the world to shame the wise. Again there was a restoration of the truth. Through this small group, so ignorant of God's will and ways, the intricacies of a sanctuary system were given so that the world might better comprehend the mighty plan of salvation. Did Moses teach something new and different, something that had never been understood by anyone prior to his time? Never! His work was a restoration of truth.

Hebrews, chapter 11, after speaking of these examples and others, reaches a pinnacle in verse 13: "These all died in faith, not having received the promises, but having seen them afar off, and were persuaded of them, and embraced them, and confessed that they were strangers and pilgrims on the earth." These were the unique ones, the different ones, the untouchables, and the rejected. These were the square pegs in round holes. Why? Because by faith they believed in God's salvation and truth.

But the most "unique" and "exclusive" figure in all history was none other than Jesus Christ. Here was the One, the only One, through whom people could be saved (see Acts 4:12). Tragically, even this basic claim is being surrendered by many Christian thought leaders today. Years ago, the ecumenical movement embraced non-Christian religions, and now many Christians feel it is too narrow to believe that only through Jesus Christ can humans be saved and that no other religion outside of Christianity is valid in itself. Thus the claims of Christ Himself are set aside as too exclusive.

Did Jesus teach anything new and original when He was on earth? According to Ellen White, He did not. "Christ was the originator of all the ancient gems of truth. Through the work of the enemy these truths had been displaced. They had been disconnected from their true position, and placed in the framework of error. Christ's work was to readjust and establish the precious gems in the framework of truth. The principles of truth which had been given by Himself to bless the world had, through Satan's agency, been buried and had apparently become extinct. Christ rescued them from the rubbish of error, gave them a new, vital force, and commanded them to shine as precious jewels, and stand fast forever."[1]

Note this. Christ's work was to "readjust and establish . . . in the framework of truth" precious gems of spiritual knowledge that He Himself had originated and given in the beginning. In the same statement, she further states that these gems of truth had been "cast . . . into the minds and thoughts of each generation." Every religion has some truth in it, but all truth originates with Christ.

As we know, the visible church became saturated with error shortly after the death of the early apostles. But God had a faithful remnant who were nurtured in the wilderness. The sixteenth-century Reformation attempted to revive the specialness and uniqueness of God's message, and succeeded remarkably well considering the circumstances under which it labored. But as the Reformation continued, it fragmented, and to a great degree remained buried under the rubbish of men's philosophies. Even recovered truths lost their former gleam.

Finally, God's prophetic clock struck the hour for the birth of the Advent movement. It was never His intention for the Advent movement to disintegrate, but following the great disappointment and its aftermath, little remained of the Millerite cause apart from Seventh-day Adventists.

The concept of uniqueness

One major point needs to be reemphasized: the uniqueness of any of God's special movements during the course of history has not consisted in newness or originality, but rather in a *rediscovery and restoration* of truth that has always existed!

The quality of uniqueness and originality has a hypnotic fascination for many minds, as underscored by the continuing craze for antiques and original paintings and the fabulous amounts of money being paid for them today. This same urge for original items has somehow spilled over into the world of religion and especially into Adventism. We Adventists seem to find a special security or sense of self-worth if we can feel that we have some teaching or doctrine that no other religious group has or ever had. True, certain prophetic aspects of God's special movements in history could be labeled unique and original, but in principle, these movements should be classified as restorative rather than innovative.

Noah's ark was certainly an original (and some are still searching for it today)! But the essence of Noah's message centered on the great and ageless theme of salvation by faith alone in the Lord.

Thus, it is the restoration concept that constitutes our uniqueness. The weeping prophet, Jeremiah, emphasized this point in his day when Judah had backslidden far from God's truth. The Lord said through him, "Stand at the crossroads and look; ask for the ancient paths, ask where the good way is, and walk in it, and you will find rest for your souls" (Jer. 6:16, NIV).

Two factors stand out clearly in this admonition: "ancient paths" and "rest for your souls." God did not instruct Jeremiah to direct Judah to a new path, but to old paths. His was a message of restoration of neglected and forgotten truths.

This was the same work that Jesus sought to accomplish during His time here on earth. He invited people to take His yoke and burden—to learn of Him—promising that the result would be rest to their souls. Was Jesus offering the people something new or different from what Jeremiah had offered? Not at all! Jesus was giving them old paths.

The comprehensiveness factor

It is not just one particular doctrine or concept of belief that is involved in the uniqueness of this movement. It is an entire pattern of thinking and believing based on God's Word. In the last days of earth, when God's restoration and reformation movement is destined to spread around the world, a most important element is the comprehensiveness factor. When all the doctrines of this church are considered as a whole, one can see that God has led us into the most comprehensive, all-inclusive, perfect system of doctrines on earth. It's a golden chain of truth, at the center of which stands Jesus Christ and Him crucified. When properly understood and practiced, this message brings meaning to life and a sense of direction, commitment, destiny. It is not a piece of truth here and there, but an entire system that in its fullness is incomparable.

We must ever be aware that the idea that "we have the truth" can be so easily perverted. On this razor-thin line we can easily lose our balance and fall off on the side of selfish exclusivism, which generates feelings of pride and superiority, or we can fall on the other side and blur the uniqueness of our message and mission by attempting to dilute and ameliorate our doctrines. Above all, we need to understand clearly that our mission and message are unique not because of who we are but because of who God is and what His Word says. We become unique as a visible church only as we submit to Him, His truth, His Word. Only then will God be pleased to use us in reaching the world with more abundant life.

The uniqueness of Sabbath

What are the truths that comprise this system of restoration and uniqueness? Probably the most prominent of these is the seventh-day Sabbath. Although God's restored truth involves more than the knowledge of the Sabbath, this aspect has always been a major part of the Seventh-day Adventism's message. History reveals seventh-day Sabbathkeeping by individuals and groups in different parts of the world, but it is the Lord's plan to restore this magnificent truth on a worldwide basis. This church constitutes the major Sabbathkeeping group. We stand virtually alone among worldwide religious groups in believing that God created the world in seven literal days and that the earth was buried by a Genesis flood. Note that I said "worldwide," for other groups here and there agree with us, but among entire church bodies represented in nearly every country of the world who believe in a literal interpretation of Genesis unfortunately we virtually have the field alone. We wish it were otherwise.

Peter, through inspiration, knew that belief in the biblical record of Creation and the Flood would be given up in the last days (see 2 Pet. 3:3-6). Most Christian churches have attempted to accommodate so-called scientific opinion of earth's origins by accepting variations of the interpretations of the geologic column and attempting to harmonize Scripture with these theories. If accepted, these accommodations discredit the seven-day Creation formula and ultimately destroy the necessity for a seventh-day Sabbath memorial of Creation. There are even some among us who favor interpreting Scripture in light of scientific research. Yet actually, neither the evolutionary model with its various interpretations nor the Creation model can be demonstrably proved. Regardless of what one believes relative to the origin of our world, it must rest largely on faith. I am convinced that in the near future our faith will be more severely tested in this area. Genetic engineering and the shaping of life in the laboratory will challenge the scriptural account of God creating human beings.

Sad to say, not all such attacks against our belief in the Seventh-day Sabbath will come from without. Nor should we be amazed when other pillars of our faith, not now under attack, are weakened by those we would expect to defend them. The eternal attack on the Sabbath and the biblical record of Creation, although not openly manifest at present, is one I predict will become increasingly evident. We will have to face it squarely. Satan is violently angry and will stop at nothing to abort this movement that has been called to preach the three angels' messages, including the first angel's call to worship God as Creator.

This first angel also commands the preaching of the everlasting gospel, but the gospel must be preached within the framework of biblical creationism and the seventh-day Sabbath, or our message will lose the brilliant power and glory that God designs for it.

When God raised up this movement at the end of the prophetic 2,300-year period, Satan already had his plans well formulated to subvert it. As an ardent student of the Scriptures (and, I might add, a believer in the year-day principle), he had the time prophecies mastered long before nineteenth-century Adventists existed. When the Sabbath and its links to Creation week began to be preached, Satan diverted people's minds in a very clever manner. Charles Darwin wrote his first draft of *Origin of Species* in 1844 and published it several years later. This work changed the thinking of the scientific world almost overnight. The very basis of the socialistic system that has dominated Eastern Europe until recently can be traced to a meeting of Karl Marx and Friedrich Engels in Paris in 1844. Thus science and politics combined have swept the world with an atheistic, evolutionary theory. The very element God used in making the Sabbath His memorial of Creation—time—is the same element Satan used in creating the evolutionary theory. The underlying basis of evolutionary thinking is that given enough time, anything can happen!

Sabbath and righteousness by faith

Many in our own ranks do not fully understand the power and beauty of the Sabbath truth. The following quotation by Ellen White says something unusual about the importance of the Sabbath: "Elder K knows not of what spirit he is. He is uniting his influence with the dragon host to oppose those who keep the commandments of God, and who have warfare before him. As far as the Sabbath is concerned, he occupies the same position as the Seventh Day Baptists."[2]

Is there a difference between the Sabbath as understood and taught by Seventh-day Adventists and as given by Seventh Day Baptists? I believe there is. Ellen White continues: "Separate the Sabbath from the messages, and it loses its power; but when connected with the message of the third angel, a power attends it which convicts unbelievers and infidels, and brings them out with strength to stand, to live, grow, and flourish in the Lord."[3] The key point is this: the relationship of the seventh-day Sabbath to the three angels' messages is the everlasting gospel. And the focal point of the everlasting gospel is the cross. The cross, then, is central to all three messages.

The emphasis of the three angels' messages, and especially the third, is righteousness by faith alone in Jesus Christ. Nothing reaches so deep into the inner recesses of a person's soul as a sense of the pardoning love of Jesus. When this is understood and experienced, obedience to all of God's will, including the seventh-day Sabbath, is the natural response. This is why we are admonished repeatedly to lift up Jesus and Him crucified before the world. Seventh-day Adventists must preach the seventh-day Sabbath in the context of the three angels' messages. People must understand the relationship between a call to worship God as Creator, memorialized by the seventh-day Sabbath, and the everlasting gospel, which has the cross as its center. Otherwise the Sabbath doctrine loses its power. When Christ and His cross occupy their rightful position, the heart is filled with an intense desire not merely to submit to but to joyfully seek God's will. Love for a person—not a doctrine, an institution, a policy book, a method, a theological or philosophical concept, or a budget—exists in the heart. Commandment keeping becomes a happy experience. The law is no longer odious or burdensome.

Thus, the true everlasting gospel, the Sabbath, and the other nine commandments of God are inseparable. The Reformers, as remarkable as they were, did not quite capture this wholistic plan of salvation. One of the unique, special privileges (and responsibilities) God has given to this people is the restoration of the Sabbath truth in the context of the everlasting gospel and the three angels' messages. There is no other religious movement on earth that has this concept in the way that we have. In that sense we have a special and unique message.

The gifts of the Spirit

The next teaching of Adventism that I wish to discuss in the setting of uniqueness is the teaching of the gifts of the Spirit, and in particular the gift of prophecy. Obviously, I am doing so since this doctrine has been and is under considerable discussion. Any religious movement that claims to have the gift of prophecy and announces that there is a prophet among that people is suspect at best. There has probably been more misunderstanding on the part of those outside the Adventist Church regarding this doctrine than any other. I don't know of an article or book written in opposition to us that does not dedicate a portion to contending against the idea of the gift of prophecy as evidenced in the writings of Ellen G. White. Furthermore, I know of no leading Seventh-day Adventist dissident, past or present, who has not used disbelief in all or part of the writings of Ellen White as a point of departure. Canright and Kellogg are just two examples; the list could be made much longer.

My heart is saddened to see confusion and dismay on the part of a few of our ministers over recent discussions on this subject. I trust that what follows may help to clarify our thinking.

I, for one, am sympathetic with those who are having problems in this area, even though I am not in agreement with them. I want to state categorically that it is my belief that church leadership, including myself, must bear a portion of the responsibility for the problems we now face in this area. As I see it, I have, consciously or unconsciously, made claims for and demands on the writings of Ellen White that exceed those I made on the writings of the Bible prophets. I have held to what might be called verbal inspiration for her writings, but not for the Scriptures. I did not do so intentionally, of course; rather, it resulted from illogical thinking. I am ashamed today to recall the many sermons I have preached based on a statement from her works in which I hammered away at a phrase or even at a single word such as "all" or "everyone" or "none."

In my college sophomore year a teacher whom I greatly appreciated brought up a point that caused me to ask him after class whether he knew of any contradictory statements or concepts in the writings of Ellen White. He hesitated several moments and finally shook his head saying, "No." This answer greatly strengthened my confidence in the prophetic gift. Being a young man, my impetuous mind, youthful dogmatism, and unrealistic idealism demanded perfection—absolute perfection—of Ellen White's writings. It was unthinkable to me to conceive of mistakes or contradictions in either the Bible or her work.

I finished my last two years of college at another campus. While there, I learned that the teacher who had told me he knew of no contradictions in Ellen White's writings had left the church! The main reason? Certain "contradictory" statements regarding chronology had rendered null and void the entire scope of her writings for him. Here again is another exhibit of a person finding fault with the gift of prophecy and departing from us.

In looking back on this experience, I have often wondered whether this teacher was already having problems in his own mind and graciously refrained from revealing his true feelings to me in order not to shake my confidence. How much better it would have been (and would be today) if we had been taught differently regarding the doctrine of inspiration and revelation, if we had understood that inspiration results in infallibility, integrity, consistency, and trustworthiness, but not necessarily in absolute personal perfection!

We should understand and teach that nowhere in Scripture do we find the doctrine of verbal inspiration or the idea of divine dictation. If God's thoughts are so much higher than our thoughts as the heavens are higher than the earth, surely we can expect a perfection of expression on the part of God that all the prophets put together could not match. And if they did, we poor mortals couldn't understand it anyway! The inerrancy debate that consumes much time and attention among some Christians today could be resolved quickly if we clearly understood that while it is true that God-inspired writings have a beauty of unity, cohesion, and oneness, and while it is true that they are infallible in concept and truthfulness as a whole, one cannot take a word, phrase, or sentence and build a concept cathedral that is contrary to the underlying harmony or theme of the whole. I feel it is most urgent and important for us as Seventh-day Adventist ministers to have a far deeper and broader understanding of the inspiration process.

I confess, too, that I have spent more time in spiritual studies reading Ellen White's words than the Bible. I did the very thing she strongly admonishes us not to do. But after saying this, let me assure you that I make no apologies for reading more of her works than those of any uninspired author, past or present!

Also, I have at times equated inspiration with originality. To make originality a test for the authenticity of inspired revelations ultimately leads to disillusionment the moment one finds a passage or pages in inspired writings that have previously appeared in noninspired documents.

In college I knew that Ellen White used material from other sources in her book, *Sketches From the Life of Paul.* No great issue was made of it, so I gave it little thought. It is interesting in this connection to note that if a loyal, spiritually mature person presents a problem such as this and attempts to provide a solution in a sweet, Christian spirit, the situation is quite readily understood and accepted. But when a problem of this nature is presented in a controversial setting as an attack on Ellen White, then it shocks people, and doubts and darkness invade the minds of some. So much depends on whether one speaks as a friend or as an enemy. Would to God there were more of a spirit of loyalty, love, and oneness among us.

Inspiration, revelation, and originality

I have had to change drastically my own thinking and attitudes on this matter of equating inspiration and revelation with originality. This change of concept came to me about 10 years ago. In the early 1970s we enlarged *Ministry* to include a sizable health section, in which we published, at times, pertinent Ellen White-written health materials under the heading "Profiting From His Prophet." One selection dealt with the importance and necessity of exercise. In response to this particular article, one reader wrote a rather lengthy letter admonishing us not to use the word "prophet" in connection with Ellen White since, in his opinion, the term indicated originality and newness, and many health concepts given by Mrs. White can be found in earlier writers.

His letter caused me to reflect on this point of originality. Frankly, at that point I was of the same opinion as he—that to be a prophet implied originality. After some study I changed my mind (see *Ministry*, May 1973).

Because of my change of mind at that time, I have had little difficulty with charges that Ellen White was a plagiarist or evidence of her literary borrowing. As things stand today, it makes little difference to me how much she borrowed or didn't borrow. Who am I to question how God uses His messengers or how His messengers obtain the right words and phrases to reveal truth—or perhaps I should say to *restore* His truth—to us today?

Today I stand in awe and appreciation as never before for what the gift of prophecy through Ellen White has meant to me personally and to this church. We have been uniquely blessed by these inspired writings. Unfortunately, we have too often ignored them, misused them, misunderstood them, or ridiculed them.

Our responsibility as Seventh-day Adventist ministers is to use them correctly and to share with our people a better understanding of revelation and inspiration.

---

1   Manuscript 25, 1890, pp. 5-7.
2   *Testimonies*, vol. 1, p. 337.
3   *Ibid.*

Chapter 11

Becoming a Member of God's Family

In recent years a rather interesting phenomenon has come about that can be summed up in one word—*roots*. Alex Haley's book by that title became a best seller and a renowned TV attraction. Haley persuasively tells the story of the search for his own family roots, which eventually led him to a small African village and his ancestors. Haley's search has led many to search their roots and to learn about their ancestors. It is even more important to know our spiritual roots and why being a member of God's family should be our greatest desire.

The first step to membership in God's family of redeemed sons and daughters is to recognize our utterly helpless and fallen condition. In fact, *on our own* we cannot even desire salvation. We may selfishly desire a happy time forever in heaven, and certainly no one in their right mind wants to suffer eternal death. But we are incapable of really desiring to be members of God's family unless the Holy Spirit creates this desire in us.

Originally Adam and Eve were created perfect—they had not the slightest inclination toward thinking or doing evil. Then came the fall, changing sin*less* beings to sin*ful* beings. For us the awful part is that when Adam sinned, he sawed off the limb on which he was sitting, and all his descendants have fallen with him. It seems unfair, but that is reality. Life produces its own kind. Spiders do not produce butterflies, nor do sinful parents produce sinless children. Furthermore, since that sorry day in Eden, all the descendants of Adam have proved this point by *themselves* sinning. Paul expresses it this way: "Sin entered the world through one man, and death through sin, and in this way death came to all men, because all sinned" (Rom. 5:12, NIV). All have sinned! The created beings that God designed for such a marvelous potential have become failures and sinners. Now, the question arises: Am I not still a member of God's family, even though I am a sinner? And if so, why do I need *to become* a member of God's family?

In a sense the whole human race is God's family. Yet we on Planet Earth are the only *rebellious* members of God's universal family, which extends to myriads of populated planets that know not sin. Thus, as rebellious beings on this isolated globe, we are aliens and "foreigners to the covenants of the promise, without hope and without God in the world" (Eph. 2:12, NIV).

But God is too good to leave us in the horrible mess started by Satan's rebellion. With indescribable love, the Godhead fashioned a costly plan to restore full privileges and blessings to the alienated family.

An inside change

With this brief introduction as a background, we shall note a few important steps to becoming a restored member of God's family. Such restoration must of necessity effect a change in our attitude and nature, not merely outwardly, but deep within. The Saviour once skillfully used a dishwashing illustration to make this point. "You clean the outside of the cup and dish, but inside they are full of greed and self-indulgence." To drive home His point more forcefully He continued, "In the same way, on the outside you appear to people as righteous but on the inside you are full of hypocrisy and wickedness." His solution? "First clean the inside of the cup and dish, and then the outside also will be clean" (Matt. 23:25, 28, 26, NIV).

So with rebellious humanity: our inner nature, the roots, must be changed before the outside is truly changed. This change is the central theme of the seal-of-God doctrine. God puts His seal, His stamp of approval, only on the person who allows Him to make this change in the life. Many doubt that such a change is possible. Many others do not want to submit to such a change. Thus both the doubting and the resisting try to invent doctrines that they hope will restore them to the family of God without being changed.

Such was the attitude of the rich young ruler whose nature needed changing before he could qualify for God's kingdom. In fact, his problem was so severe that the Lord said, "It is easier for a camel to go through the eye of a needle than for a rich man to enter the kingdom of God." How did the disciples respond? "They were greatly astonished and asked, 'Who then can be saved?'" In other words, is it possible for human nature to be changed? The answer Jesus gave was positive and wonderfully encouraging. He said, "With man this is impossible, but with God all things are possible" (Matt. 19:23-26, NIV).

It is God's work

"With God all things are possible." This is the key to salvation. This short, pithy statement contains several important basic truths. First, it tells us that salvation centers not on human beings, but on God. It is *God's* work, not ours. The true way of salvation is by grace through faith in Christ. The Lord is the one who does the saving. Now, we have established two principles on which to build. The first is that our nature is degraded and needs to be changed. The second is that change is possible, as Jesus plainly stated. "With God all things are possible."

There is no equivocation regarding the necessity of this change. Jesus told Nicodemus plainly that he "must be born again" (John 3:7). The word *must* is nonnegotiable; there is no way around it. The new birth and eternal life are inseparable. This is not a popular truth, but it is the unalterable prerequisite for entrance into the family of God.

Ever remember that the changing of our nature is *God's* work, not ours. God is the initiator of the whole salvation process. The touching parable of the shepherd with one lost sheep illustrates this point. Jesus asks His listeners, "Does he not leave the ninety-nine in the open country and go after the lost sheep until he finds it?" (Luke 15:4, NIV). Jesus is the Shepherd—we are the lost sheep. God makes the first move to find us. Too many discouraged people, lost sheep, feel they must help the Shepherd find them. They must repent or be good *before* God's love is extended to them. Jesus tried to dispel this terribly mistaken concept, and in so doing was criticized by the church leaders, who sneeringly said, "This man welcomes sinners and eats with them" (Luke 15:2, NIV).

Why is this point so important? If a person has the idea that he must change *before* he comes to God, either he will never come or he will come on his own terms. He will attempt to make himself worthy to come to God. That is what we call salvation by works, and it is at the heart of the system symbolized by the beast in Revelation 13. This system teaches that we can earn the right to come to God—we deserve to be in His family. This is the exact opposite of the truth. If we miss the point that God is the one who initiates the action to save us, then the whole plan of salvation makes no sense and is utterly destroyed. A change in our lives is impossible until we capture this concept and understand it thoroughly. No matter how wicked a person has been, the Saviour is seeking for him. And when the Good Shepherd finds him, bruised, bleeding, and wounded, He takes him tenderly into His arms and with great joy carries him back to the fold of safety. What a magnificent Saviour we have!

Because our Lord took the first step to save us, any desire to be a member of His family and to submit ourselves to Him comes from the Saviour Himself, not from us. It is absolutely impossible for a sinner to be lost if he does not resist the magnetic drawing power of Jesus. We are predestined, if you please, to be saved. There is no favoritism with God. Only our own stubbornness and willfulness can keep us from Christ. If we choose not to resist, we will be drawn to Him.

Our choice

When a person makes that choice (a choice that itself is a result of the Holy Spirit's work), he is given the spirit of repentance as a gift. But remember, even before we repent Jesus is drawing us. If a person looks to Jesus and accepts the repentance God offers, he is well on the road to becoming a restored member of God's family. It is probably at this point more than any other that most failures in becoming and remaining a member of the Lord's family occur. It is difficult for the human heart to accept its helplessness and depend solely on Someone else.

This point is made in a variety of ways throughout the Scriptures. Jesus underscored this principle to Nicodemus in John 3:14, 15: "And as Moses lifted up the serpent in the wilderness, even so must the Son of man be lifted up, that whosoever believeth in him should not perish, but have eternal life." His illustration was taken from the story of the brass serpent in the wilderness. The meaning was clear: There was no healing virtue in the brass object itself; it was the person's faith in God and His word that made the difference. Believing in God's word, obeying His command by looking in faith, emancipated the sick person from death. The real "fight of faith" that Paul speaks of in 1 Timothy 6:12 comes at this point. Will we look to Jesus, or will we look at self?

The lessons of John 3:14, 15 are so obvious that I will enumerate only a few:
1. The wound of sin cannot be healed by any works the sinner tries to perform.
2. There is no scientific basis for healing by looking.
3. Even though we may not be able to arrange the steps of salvation chronologically, the first giant step is to look by faith to Jesus.
4. All attempts to be saved other than by lifting up Jesus in the wilderness of our own heart and looking in faith to Him are fatal.
5. Like Nicodemus, who learned the lesson well, we must search the Scriptures in a way that leads us to Christ as the center of salvation.
6. Controversy regarding the logic or necessity of God's plan of salvation leads to death, not life. Rather, there is life in looking to Him.
7. Look not to self with all of its defects and wounds, but rely on the merits of Christ alone, and the help we need will be ours. If we look at the snakebites of sin, we will only get worse and die.
8. Do not wait until every detail of salvation is plain before looking to Jesus. Do not continue wandering in philosophical doubts and fears. Rather, look now in simple faith to the Saviour, who became "sin for us" (2 Cor. 5:21).

The greatest battle

It sounds incredibly easy and wonderful, doesn't it? But wait a moment! The greatest battle facing every sinner is over looking to, or not looking to, Jesus. Paul employs a battle term to illustrate this point: "Fight the good fight of faith, lay hold on eternal life" (1 Tim. 6:12). The greatest struggle in the life of one who wants to become a member of the family of God is the struggle to look to Jesus by faith alone. It is so much easier to look at our trials, problems, weaknesses, husband, wife, children, money, TV, sex—the list is endless. It is much easier to *do* something rather than to *look* at something to be saved. It is much easier to doubt than to believe. It is much easier to study the Bible for information rather than for inspiration and salvation. And so the poor human race struggles on in doubts, fears, and perplexities, waiting to die from its wounds rather than fighting "the good fight of faith." Look to Jesus!

What causes us to look to Jesus? My only answer is the working of the Holy Spirit, the third Person of the Godhead. Nothing precedes the Holy Spirit's work. I cannot even desire to look to Jesus unless the Spirit causes me to. When I, at the instigation of the Spirit, look to Jesus, the goodness of God leads me to repent (Rom. 2:4). Repentance is not the result of my own decision. When I look to Jesus, I will humbly confess my sins and make restitution as far as possible. When I look to Jesus, I will take delight in obeying His will. When I look to Him, I will long for purity of mind and heart. Looking to Jesus means more than merely "life in a look," because I must keep looking to Him as long as my heart beats. All this is the work of the Holy Spirit, who draws me always to look to Jesus.

Perhaps the finest example in Scripture of true repentance is that of King David, who committed the double crime of murder and adultery. I have memorized his great prayer of repentance, found in Psalm 51, and I urge you to memorize it, too. David begs God for mercy; he acknowledges his sins; he pleads for cleansing; he beseeches God to create in him a clean heart and to renew a right spirit within him. He appeals for the presence of the Holy Spirit to remain with him and asks for restoration to the joy of salvation. Finally David proclaims the goodness of God and His righteousness. Take your Bible, and on your knees study this psalm reverently. Ask God to do for you what He did for David. Perhaps you have not, like David, committed such terrible sins as adultery and murder, but any sin can destroy your relationship with the Lord and keep you from becoming a member of His family.

I urge you to take the little book *Steps to Christ* and repeatedly read this precious volume that persuasively and tenderly outlines confession, restitution, consecration, discipleship, and growing up into Christ.

Salvation, like an automobile, comes in a package. If it is to have any meaning or function at all, then it must remain as a package. Remove the engine, clutch, spark plugs, or fuel pump from a car and you do not have an automobile any longer. It may *look* like a car, but it does not *function* as a car. So with salvation. Remove or ignore any part of God's plan to save men and women, and you may have people going about who look like Christians, and even claim to be Christians, but do not function as Christians.

Justification is the primary, or foundational, basis for our salvation. But ever remember that—although justification cannot be earned by works, although it is what God does for the sinner, although it is not a mingling of God's work with our work, although it changes our status with God, although it is God's verdict, not our achievement, although it is the basis of our assurance and acceptance with God, although it includes pardon and forgiveness for past sin—justification is never given to us as a gift by itself. God's love is greater than that.

The core of His gift is justification, but along with it comes a change, a new-birth experience, and then a lifelong walk with God that we call sanctification. Justification settles our present account, but it also applies to our future as a covering umbrella from the moment we accept Christ until we meet the Lord. Nevertheless, anyone who leaves sanctification out of the plan of salvation and focuses only on justification is like a used car salesperson trying to sell a car without brakes or steering mechanism. Not only does God do something *for* us, He also does something *in* us.

But above and beyond all is the fact that God is the one who initiates, maintains, and consummates the entire salvation process. He is drawing us back to our roots, back to His original plan for us, back to harmony with Himself, back to the family of heaven. We cannot restore ourselves. We can only cooperate with Him as He restores us. In every aspect of our salvation it is God who is working. He only wants from us our cooperation.

Chapter 12

The Church on Fire

Who would deny the need of kindling a spiritual fire in our organization? The recurring symbolism attached to fire in the Scriptures is worthy of study. The Trinity is described in terms relative to fire and its effects. Deuteronomy 4:24 declares, "The Lord thy God is a consuming fire." God's revelation of Himself in a burning bush deeply impressed Moses with the purity and power of God. When the Lord communed with Moses on the heights of Sinai He "descended upon it in fire: and the smoke thereof ascended as the smoke of a furnace, and the whole mount quaked greatly" (Ex. 19:18). "Out of heaven he made thee to hear his voice, that he might instruct thee: and upon earth he shewed thee his great fire" (Deut. 4:36). The awful grandeur of this scene of flame and smoke upheld the authority and dignity of God's written character—the Ten Commandments.

In describing the Lord's form, Daniel records that His face was "as the appearance of lightning, and his eyes as lamps of fire" (Dan. 10:6). John's description compares Christ's eyes to a "flame of fire" and His feet to "pillars of fire" (Rev. 1:14; 10:1). Our Saviour is referred to as "a refiner's fire" (Mal. 3:2). These descriptions are in harmony with the concept of the fiery pillar which guided and warmed the Israelites at night during their desert wandering.

Angels, creatures, and Word

God's angels are equated with "a flaming fire" (Ps. 104:4). Ezekiel's vision of the four living creatures was so strikingly radiant that he described them in terms of fire and lightning. "As for the likeness of the living creatures, their appearance was like burning coals of fire, and like the appearance of lamps: it went up and down among the living creatures; and the fire was bright, and out of the fire went forth lightning" (Eze. 1:13). Jeremiah quotes the Lord as saying, "Is not my word like as a fire?" (Jer. 23:29). God's promise to Jeremiah is significant. "Because ye speak this word, behold, I will make my words in thy mouth fire, and this people wood, and it shall devour them" (Jer. 5:14). The experience of this same prophet who at one time in his life declared he was finished with preaching, led him to find out the nature and influence of God's Word in his own life. "But his word was in mine heart as a burning fire shut up in my bones, and I was weary with forbearing, and I could not stay" (Jer. 20:9).

Thus one of the most used terms in connection with the description of the Godhead and their process of salvation is fire or its equivalent.

Fire symbolizes acceptance

God on various occasions expressed His acceptance of people and things by the use of fire. Fire passed through and devoured the divided pieces of heifer, goat, ram, dove, and pigeon when God made a covenant with Abraham (see Gen. 15). A glorious demonstration of fire from heaven consumed the sacrifice offered by Moses at the dedication of the tabernacle. So mighty was this experience, the Israelites "shouted, and fell on their faces" (Lev. 9:24). The parents of Samson witnessed the acceptance of their offering by a divinely ignited fire plus the ascension of the angel of the Lord in the burning flames (Jud. 13:19, 20).

Another exhibition of heavenly fire took place at the dedication of Solomon's temple. This brilliant leader had just finished his dedicatory prayer, in which he eloquently pleaded for the mercies of God. A blaze of fire issued by God's command "consumed the burnt offering and the sacrifices; and the glory of the Lord filled the house" (2 Chron. 7:1). The effects of this dynamic display of glory and power prevented the priests from entering the temple for a period of time. The impact of this scene of splendor moved the children of Israel to bow themselves with their faces to the ground, and they worshiped and praised the Lord, saying, "For he is good; for his mercy endureth for ever" (chap. 7:3).

The prophet of fire

The name of Elijah and fire are almost synonymous. The proof of the supremacy of God or Baal was based on fire. "And the God that answereth by fire, let him be God" (1 Kings 18:24). The all-consuming nature of Carmel's conflagration is revealed in the fact that water, dust, stones, wood, and sacrifices were devoured. This particular fire left no doubt in the hearts of the beholders as to who was God. "When all the people saw it, they fell on their faces; and they said 'The Lord, he is God'" (1 Kings 18:39, RSV).

The injured Ahaziah who fell from an upper chamber sent messengers to Baalzebub, the god of Ekron, to discern whether he would recover or not. God instructed Elijah to intercept these messengers with a rebuke in the form of a question. "Is it not because there is not a God in Israel, that ye go to enquire of Baalzebub the god of Ekron?" (2 Kings 1:3). The insolent demand of Ahaziah in response to this question cost the lives of 102 men. Two groups of fifty soldiers, each with a captain over them, heard their funeral oration from the lips of this prophet of fire. "If I be a man of God, then let fire come down from heaven, and consume thee and thy fifty. And there came down fire from heaven, and consumed him and his fifty" (2 Kings 1:10). There was no question about the fact that God accepted Elijah as a man of God. He proved it by fire.

Exit by fire

Elijah's exit from this earth was in a chariot of fire with horses of fire. Elijah's successor, Elisha, prayed for the eyes of his servant to behold a similar scene in Dothan. The Lord responded to this request, "and he saw: and, behold the mountain was full of horses and chariots of fire round about Elisha" (2 Kings 6:17).

Gideon was another person who entered into an enviable experience of witnessing acceptance by fire. He saw the angel of the Lord put forth the end of his staff and touch the flesh and unleavened cakes of his offering until a fire came out of the rock and consumed them (Judges 6:21).

David was asked to make the awful choice of selecting one of three punishments. This had to be done because of his own foolish action of numbering Israel, and the decision involved the lives of his people. He had to choose famine, sword, or pestilence. David choose to fall into the hands of God rather than the hands of men. At God's instruction, David built an altar and laid out the sacrifice, and God not only stayed the pestilence but "answered him from heaven by fire upon the altar of burnt offering" (1 Chron. 21:26).

Modern equivalent of acceptance by fire

In our supposedly more religiously enlightened age, experiences of acceptance by God by an outward display of fire are unknown. Yet God's acceptance is no less necessary to the church today than it was several millenniums ago. Could it be that the church should give evidence of this acceptance by exhibiting the "gold tried in the fire" (Rev. 3:18)? Could it be that a congregation that possesses this *gold of faith and love* would make the church appear as if it is on fire? Could it be that if we as ministers set the pace by dedicating our lives to the task of securing this gold tried in the fire, our members will follow our lead?

Retreat spells extinction

The fire symbolism features tremendous lessons for the church today. Fire is active, never passive. Fire must advance—retreat spells extinction. It cannot rest, it is ever moving. It sweeps, it covers, it never spares itself. Fire is never self-contained—it always shares with others. Never works by proxy. It exists by involving itself. Fire is enthusiastic, never reticent. It is unyielding in achieving its goal. Fire never plays it safe. It never stops to question but keeps on burning. To live, fire must consume. It cannot feed on nothing. Fire is concerned with one thing only—burning. It cannot be sidetracked—it burns whatever is in its path. Fire spells surrender on the part of that which burns. The result is contagious.

Born to burn

So with the witnessing church today. Put her in chains, consign her to an island, stamp on her, throw water on her, do what you will against her, but she continues to burn! This is what happened to the New Testament church. Opposition only fanned her burning into a giant conflagration which gloriously warmed the earth with the gospel of Christ. A church on fire for God is one of the most exhilarating concepts the mind can entertain. A church single-minded, constantly advancing, fully surrendered, unquenchable in spirit—this is God's plan for the Advent Movement. Would to God that the symbolism of fire be a spiritual reality in our midst. Like the sanctuary of old, may "the fire . . . ever be burning upon the altar; it shall never go out" (Lev. 6:13).

The church was born to burn!

Chapter 13

The High Cost of Prejudice

With all our present-day education and enlightenment, prejudice is far from being wiped out. Racial and ethnic prejudice may supply us with prepackaged opinions and ready-made labels for other people, but the cost is high. In Christ's day, both Jews and Samaritans were indulging in this expensive practice. Through centuries of hostility, rooted in imagined and real slights, snubbings, competition, and outright violence, these two groups of people kept their distance. In actuality, however, they held many similar beliefs and practices. Both accepted Moses' writings and treasured sacred copies of his five books, and both worshiped in temples dedicated to Jehovah. Both believed in a coming Messiah. However, each group avoided contact with the other whenever possible, outside of market transactions.

In the time of Jesus, most Jews traveling north from Jerusalem to Galilee refused to set foot on the intervening Samaritan territory and would even detour across the Jordan River. Ellen White observes, "A Jew would not borrow from a Samaritan, nor receive a kindness, not even a morsel of bread or a cup of water. The disciples, in buying food, were acting in harmony with the custom of their nation. But beyond this they did not go. To ask a favor of the Samaritans, or in any way seek to benefit them, did not enter into the thought of even Christ's disciples."[1] Not so with Jesus; He did not bypass Samaria. One day when thirsty He sat near Jacob's well to wait for someone to draw water. A woman came to get water, and He asked her gently, "Give me to drink" (John 4:7).

I have often wondered what made the woman sure Jesus was a Jew. John simply says she asked, "How is it that thou, being a Jew, askest drink of me, which am a woman of Samaria?" (verse 9). At Nablus, near the site of Jacob's well, I have talked to some of the few remaining Samaritans and photographed them. Although they have not married outside their group through most of their history, in their features and skin color they certainly do not differ noticeably from Jews. Yet "the woman saw that Jesus was a Jew."[2]

What did she see—a difference in His dress or perhaps in His dialect? At any rate she knew, and He, of course, knew what she was. More than that, both were aware of the deep feelings of prejudice that existed between the two groups.

Prejudice is something anyone can have. Not only are people born with predispositions toward sin and against righteousness, but as they learn to walk and talk they develop other prejudices of many sorts, often reflecting the attitudes prevalent in their families or social groups. Some develop more intolerant attitudes than do others. Those who are converted to Christ and make progress in the Christian pathway have the strongest incentives to discard feelings of superiority and to accept others as children of God.

A form of bondage

Because prejudice restricts clear thinking and opinions, it is really a form of bondage. Today much of the world trusts to inbred prejudices and hatreds to guide its treatment of others. With all our present-day education and enlightenment, prejudice is far from wiped out. Ellen White surprises us with this statement: "Prejudice is even stronger in the hearts of men now than in Christ's day."[3]

Jesus' excursion with the disciples into Samaria was His first major training session for His disciples in the art of overcoming prejudice. It was also His first major attempt to help people in a minority group to eliminate prejudice from their hearts, as well. It is a beautiful and significant story. A member of a minority group and people belonging to a majority group were for the first time being brought together in the presence of the Son of God.

Jesus' main objective in talking to the Samaritan woman and others she might influence was to dispense the water of life. He made it clear to His disciples that the gospel is supreme, and its progress should be their chief concern. His dealings with the Samaritans clearly teach us, who bear the water of life for Him, that we must not permit prejudicial attitudes to limit the progress of the gospel. Anything that is allowed to do so will surely delay the accomplishment of His purposes. We handicap our church's outreach when we allow prejudice to dictate our actions toward others. We have sustained losses as a world, as a nation, and as a church because of prejudice, for discrimination has limited not only the freedom of people to develop their true potential but also their attitude toward the God whom the church represents.

Jesus' tactful words at the well were designed to help the Samaritan woman overcome her prejudice against Jews. In speaking them, however, He did not compromise the claims of the gospel nor soft-pedal truth. When she referred to the longstanding disagreement over the place of worship, Jesus plainly declared, "Ye worship ye know not what: we know what we worship: for salvation is of the Jews" (John 4:22). He was referring to the fact that the Samaritans' faith was corrupted with traces of idolatry and concern for external details, while the great truths of redemption had been committed to the Jews, among whom the Messiah would appear. The Lord proceeded to lift the woman's mind above terms, concepts, or labels. He wanted her to understand that "the hour cometh, and now is, when the true worshipers shall worship the Father in spirit and in truth: for the Father seeketh such to worship him" (4:23).

God is still seeking true worshipers today. He is trying to lift our minds above differences, above the concept that some races and nationalities are superior to others, above jealousies and prejudices, to a grand and glorious experience of worshiping in spirit and truth. The central theme of the first angel's message is "Worship Him." The Father actively seeks for true worshipers and is willing to work wonders in the lives of those who respond. The Samaritan woman did respond, and her attitude changed as though by a miracle. Any person who permits God to have His way in the heart can similarly experience this freedom from the bondage of prejudice. E. E. Cleveland expresses it beautifully in his little book *The Middle Wall*: "The gospel has done its work. In the woman's sight the Jew has become a man. 'How can you, being a Jew' is changed to 'Come, see a man.' She has completed the cycle from racial intransigence to Christian love. No genuine Christian will settle for less" (page 23).

We could wish that the disciples who witnessed Christ's unprejudiced, tactful approach to the Samaritan woman would have been as swift to comprehend as she was. We are told, "The stay of Jesus in Samaria was designed to be a blessing to His disciples, who were still under the influence of Jewish bigotry. They felt that loyalty to their own nation required them to cherish enmity toward the Samaritans. They wondered at the conduct of Jesus. They could not refuse to follow His example, and during the two days in Samaria, fidelity to Him kept their prejudices under control; yet in heart they were unreconciled. They were slow to learn that their contempt and hatred must give place to pity and sympathy. But after the Lord's ascension, His lessons came back to them with a new meaning."[4]

Evil effects of prejudice

We need today to grasp a new revelation of God's love. If we could really see the whole picture of sin and rebellion, beginning in heaven and continuing on earth, we could appreciate what God meant when He said He had known "good and evil" (Gen. 3:22). To be treated as an object and not as a person is a painful experience, and that is how God must have felt when Lucifer became jealous and turned the hearts of the angels against Him.

Human inhumanity to fellow humans became such an expected part of human nature that Jesus had to come to the earth as a human being to show us what true humanity, our real destiny, can be like. He witnessed the evil effects of prejudice at every step in His life, from the attempt of Herod to destroy Him as a babe to the taunts of the Pharisees and soldiers as He hung on the cross. Yet He had an answer for it.

Those who really search for Christ's way "in spirit and in truth" will experience this revelation. It will not only free them individually from the shackles of racial and ethnic prejudice but will greatly enhance their service to the church. When enough people see Him in His true beauty, minority church members will not feel forced to protest for their racial pride and press for recognition, nor will there be "advantaged" segments of the church that strive to ensure their privileged position. All will view each other as individual children of the same Father and deserving of equal love and regard.

Price of prejudice too high

The price of prejudice has been too high—for the kingdom of God and for the church. We cannot afford it now, for it is a major obstacle to the progress of the gospel. Whether it be prejudice springing from resentment or from pride, may

God help us to see it for what it is, and conquer it. When we do away with it in our hearts and our institutions, we can begin to get on with the real business of proclaiming the gospel to the world.

It often happens, unfortunately, that our feelings tell us we are *right* in denying others their potential for growth and service for Christ. We must be especially on guard against these feelings, for they come from other sources than the Spirit of Christ. What we need to do is cultivate every bit of capacity with which we have been endowed to love God and our fellow Christians. We dare not permit anything to destroy that capacity.

Our only safety is in looking unto Jesus. Study His handling of human relations. Watch with Him in prayer for unity among His people. Look at Him on the cross, a victim of prejudice-distorted "righteous" Pharisaism. Make certain on a daily basis that we are fully committed to Him. In *Don Quixote*, Cervantes expresses the thought that people have two inalienable rights: sovereignty in their home and exclusivity in their marriage. I would like to add a third, expressed not by Cervantes but by God. He says, "Son, give me thine heart" (Prov. 23:2, 6). This is God's inalienable right—to possess our lives. To deny Him this is to deny the very basis of life itself. In accepting His supremacy in our lives we do not lose, but gain. We become His sons and daughters, with rights and privileges that are guaranteed to us forever.

When our Lord cried out upon the cross, "It is finished," He proclaimed the ultimate end of inhumanity. He makes men truly *human*, not by force, but by His love. And that love is the defeat of prejudice. Prejudice is now destined to be forever wiped from the universe. Love will be enthroned. None will ever dispute God's reign over the heart of mankind, for that reign was purchased by the blood of His Son. "I, if I be lifted up from the earth, will draw all men unto me" (John 12:32). All will agree that the price of prejudice was far too high.

Can we look with unwavering gaze at that uplifted cross and let it neutralize the poison of prejudice while it draws us to Him? Perhaps we can then be a help and not a hindrance to men and women who also want to look.

---

1   *The Desire of Ages*, p. 183.
2   *Ibid.*, p. 184.
3   *Ibid.*, p. 587.
4   *Ibid.*, pp. 193, 194.

Chapter 14

Laodicea

How does Christ size up Laodiceans? "I know thy works, that thou art neither cold nor hot: I would thou wast cold or hot" (Rev. 3:15). This one sentence, if true, and it is, shocks the mind to even consider its meaning. Christ here states a tremendous preference. He prefers that men and women should declare themselves in earnest either for Him or against Him. Can this be true? Lukewarmness or indifference, when it comes to salvation, is the worst thing possible. Lukewarmness on the part of the person who claims to be a servant of Christ is inexcusable. The lukewarm Christian is like a marsh, bubbling and oozing and even glistening at times, but there is a repulsive stagnation that at times carries an unpleasant odor.

The divine commentary, which is not given to flattery, states, "Halfhearted Christians are worse than infidels; for their deceptive words and noncommittal position lead many astray. The infidel shows his colors. The lukewarm Christian deceives both parties. He is neither a good worldling nor a good Christian. Satan uses him to do a work that no one else can do."[1]

Revelation 3, verse 17, further interprets what this lukewarm condition is all about. "Because thou sayest, I am rich, and increased with goods, and have need of nothing; and knowest not that thou art wretched, and miserable, and poor, and blind, and naked." Note the words, "knowest not." It is almost inconceivable to think of a person wretched, miserable, poor, blind, and naked—and not being aware of that condition.

The Laodicean disease is serious

It is true that the Laodicean disease is a serious one. Poverty, nakedness, and blindness are an awful condition to be in. But this is not the most serious part of our condition. Christ has a remedy for our poverty, nakedness, and blindness, but He has *no* remedy for the "knowest not," willful, ignorant condition. This is the fatal aspect of the Laodicean disease—our total insensitivity to our condition. It is like a man with both wrists cut, blood spurting out rapidly, and as the doctor tries to help him, the patient shouts loud and long that there is absolutely nothing wrong with him—he is in excellent condition, in no need of help, the doctor is wasting his time. Yet it is only a matter of minutes before death ends it all.

Christ has a remedy for the Laodicean condition. Verse 18 makes it clear that although Laodiceans are poor, they can become rich; although naked, they can become clothed; and although blind, they are not incurably blind. Christ offers the gold of faith and love; the robe of His righteousness, which is the purity of His character, to clothe us; and the eyesalve which "is that wisdom and grace which enables us to discern between the evil and the good, and to detect sin under any guise."[2] But He offers us even more than all these blessings. Listen to this marvelous offer in Revelation 3, verse 20: "Behold, I stand at the door, and knock: if any man hear my voice, and open the door, I will come in to him, and will sup with him, and he with me." Can you imagine such love, such concern? In spite of our poverty, nakedness, and blindness, Christ stands at our heart's door seeking to come in and help us.

There are certain priorities in life that are common to all of us. A knock at the door demands for most people an immediate response. Whether we are resting, eating, scrubbing the floor, watching TV, or talking with the family, when a knock comes, we answer the door. We may not feel like answering the door, but we do. Many times we are disappointed as to who is at the door—the unwanted salesperson or perhaps a solicitor—yet we answer the door knock.

The question is, How have we responded to the Saviour's knock? I hear some say, "Well, when did He ever knock at my door?" None reading these words can honestly say, "He never knocked at my door."

Christ knocks

Christ knocks through the Word. Perhaps a phrase or sentence pierces the soul and God seeks entrance at that moment. Or a Christian friend speaks a word, offers help—a cup of cold water or just sharing his or her positiveness—and you know Christ has knocked again. Or some providential happening—being saved from accident or being brought through a serious illness—can reveal Christ. Or a way is opened when you need help desperately—Christ knocks repeatedly in this fashion.

Think of Christ taking the initiative. It is He who made the weary, dangerous trip from heaven to our doorstep. Through the wilderness of temptation, over the hills of persecution and ridicule, and finally through the valley of the shadow of death, Jesus has come that He may have the right and privilege to stand at our heart's door and knock.

Note our text declares that He not only knocks but cries out, "If any man hear my voice." Then imagine the intimate relationship Jesus offers us. He promises to come in and sit down with us and eat with us. Think of it! The Creator and Redeemer is willing to come to my home and dine with me. We would consider it an honor if the country's president notified us that he would be visiting our home for dinner some evening. We probably would never cease talking about such an experience, would we? Yet here is One, far superior to all earthly potentates, who would gladly come in to our soul home and not eat just once or twice, but room and board with us on a permanent basis!

I hear some heart cry out, Preacher, how do you open the door?

First, there must be an identifiable experience in the form of a decision to surrender or to give or to choose to let Christ have your entire being. Once a person does this, often he will find pockets of resistance still remaining in the heart. Thus we do not make that full capitulation to God. We barely crack the door. A few streams of light from the Saviour's face get through, but the being of Christ is left standing outside.

But the battle is not lost. "The warfare against self is the greatest battle that was ever fought. The yielding of self, surrendering all to the will of God, requires a struggle; but the soul must submit to God before it can be renewed in holiness."[3] Winning that battle requires a conscious choice to serve Him, a choice repeated a hundred times a day in a hundred different situations. That choice begins the moment you awaken in the morning. Will you get up in time to renew your acquaintance with Christ through prayer, meditation, and study?

Importance of study and prayer

Is there any student who believes that he can get through school successfully and secure a diploma without taking time to study? It is a foolish question, isn't it? Yet how many persons call themselves Christians, claim even the assurance of salvation, and yet day after day they never study the Word or have real prayer sessions with the Lord. Reading the Morning Watch book is good, but it is not enough. Taking a brief look at the Sabbath school lesson is good, but it is not enough. We must fill the whole heart with the words of God on a continuing basis.

One time Jesus made a startling statement to His audience. He said, "Except you eat the flesh of the Son of man, and drink his blood, ye have no life in you" (John 6:53). This was a repulsive concept to many, but He finally explained Himself by saying, "The words that I speak unto you, they are spirit, and they are life" (John 6:63).

Just as your bodies are built from what you eat and drink, so in the spiritual area, what you meditate upon gives you tone and strength in your spiritual nature. Ellen White counsels us to spend a thoughtful hour each day contemplating the life of Christ, especially the closing scenes of His life. If every person desiring to be a Christian did this faithfully, we would see a revival and reformation within a matter of days. No person can stay the same while daily dining with the Saviour.

Then when one spends this time with the Lord, automatically he will speak to others and represent Him to the world by every action. This does not mean that you have to give a Bible study to everyone you meet, but the influence of such a life constantly witnesses for Christ. In the office, in the classroom, on the hospital floors, in the factory, in the home, your whole being is a consistent testimony that God is love. Those who daily open that door for Christ to come in are the most valuable members we have. These are the ones who, like the disciples, pray with an intense earnestness for a fitness to meet men. These are the ones who carry a burden for the salvation of others.

Jesus is going from door to door, standing in front of every soul temple. He is the heavenly merchantman. He opens His treasures and blessings, and with knocking and crying out He declares, Buy of Me gold more precious than that found anywhere in the world. It has no dross, no alloy, to decrease its value. It is the gold of "faith that worketh by love." Take and wear My white raiment, which is My own robe of righteousness that took Me 33 years to weave on the loom of My earthly life's experience. Then take My oil, the oil of the Holy Spirit, and apply it to your eyes. It will give spiritual eyesight to your soul that is in blindness and darkness. Oh, open your door—transact your business with Me! It is I, your Redeemer, who counsels you. It is I, your Creator, who is willing to come in and sit down with you and have that most intimate experience of supping with you.

It is a great invitation. Beyond our comprehension. What will you do with it? How will you respond to His knocking and pleading? You and you alone determine your response.

There lived in the mountains an old, old man who was known for his superior wisdom and judgment. He had the reputation of being able to answer correctly any question put to him. One day a brilliant young man decided to prove that he could ask the old man a question that he could not answer correctly. His companions claimed that he was attempting the impossible. So he caught a bird, held it tightly in his hands, and left only the bird's tailfeathers showing. The young man's right thumb was against the live bird's neck. He took it to the old man and asked him to identify what he had in his hands. Of course, the answer was obvious, for the tailfeathers of the bird were clearly showing. The old man quickly responded, "My son, you have a bird in your hands." Then the smart young fellow asked, "Is this bird dead or alive?" Had the old man answered, "Dead," the boy would have opened his hands and let the bird fly away. Had the old man answered, "Alive," the lad had determined to snap its neck with his thumb and let it drop dead at the old man's feet. When the question was asked, the old man didn't answer for some time. He quietly gazed into the deceiving eyes of his youthful questioner, and then he finally answered, "Young man, whether that bird is dead or alive, the decision rests with you!"

Whether you wish to remain in your miserable, wretched, poor, blind, and naked state or to be rich with the gold of faith and love, to be clothed with the righteousness of Christ, to have His sight-giving eyesalve applied to your blind eyes, and finally to sit on the throne with Christ—that decision is yours.

---

1   Ellen G. White comments on Rev. 3:15, 16 in *The SDA Bible Commentary.*
2   *Testimonies*, vol. 4, pp. 88, 89.
3   *Steps to Christ,* p. 43.

Chapter 15

Adventist Amalekites

Ancient Israel had those who followed, sniping at its heels to disturb and harass. So does the church. Unity does not demand that we keep silent in the face of sin or error, but it does demand responsibility.

In today's culture, everyone wants to do their own thing and be heard. In politics, strident voices shout loud and long as to how the king, prime minster, or president ought to run the country. Unity of thought and action among any sizable group is about as rare as a penguin at the equator.

Disunity is bad enough in the political world, but tragically the intensity and confusion of life in general has spilled over into religious circles. The church is not immune to elements of discord and strife, nor is our own Seventh-day Adventist denomination. Fortunately for our church—both leadership and laity— a remarkable degree of unity and loyalty exists among the vast majority. Those in our midst whose main objective in life seems to be making waves and rocking the good ship Zion are still in the minority even if they sometimes make a dispro-portionate splash. Although their numbers, I believe, are relatively small, I am deeply concerned about this class of individuals whom I call "Adventist Amalekites."

The term *Amalekite* usually evokes thoughts of a rather fierce, offensive tribe which relentlessly caused Israel problems during their wanderings from Egypt to Canaan. After Israel's settlement in Canaan, Saul and David had to continue the fight against these inveterate enemies of God. In modern parlance, the Amalekites were the ever-present "snipers" shooting at the people of God during their struggles in the wilderness and in Canaan. According to some scholars, they were related to the Israelites through Esau. If this is correct, then in a sense they were members of the same church! These defiant people harassed God's wearied ranks until they finally sealed their doom under the judgments of God. "I will completely erase the memory of the Amalekites from under heaven" (Ex. 17:14, NIV).

Church under attack

Spiritual Israel today faces a somewhat similar situation in its journey to heaven's Canaan. God's weak, faulty, but precious church is under attack by jour-nals, books, tapes, pamphlets, magazines, and circulars of every description. Viewpoints range from the ultraconservative to the ultraliberal. Some profess great loyalty by claiming to defend the purity of the church's faith and practice. They castigate the church for abandoning what they perceive to be its original heritage. Others are obviously cynical and faith-destroying. They criticize the church for clinging to outmoded forms and failing to move into what they see as enlightened Christianity. Some of the material comes under the guise of sophisticated scholarship, while other material is quite crude in both design and content. The subject range is as broad as the church. There is virtually nothing the church stands for, in doctrine, practice, policy, or structure, that has not come under suspicion, been questioned, called upon to change, or attacked. The content is not all bad, nor is it all good. Some of it is plainly "strange fire."

Several common threads run through these productions. They claim to be speaking for and/or to the Seventh-day Adventist Church. They claim to represent Adventist thought. If not claiming to have "the truth," they claim to be searching for it. These missives also have in common a lavish treatment of the wrongs of the church and a very stingy record in offering solutions.

My concern for these critics, whether on the right or the left, is twofold: First, I am concerned for their own souls, and second, I am concerned for the souls of those who are adversely influenced by them.

I don't presume to judge the motives of these writers and speakers. Yet, looking at the materials they produce, I wonder how much time they spend praying for God's Spirit to bless this church, compared to what they expend criticizing it. Furthermore, I have wondered at times what their tithe and offering records have looked like. It would be strange indeed if one who feels so constrained to attack the church should also feel constrained to support it financially. Not that anyone's relationship to the church saves that person. But where we expend our time, energies, and financial resources certainly indicates where our interests lie.

It seems to me that those who have dedicated their lives to "setting the record straight" are jeopardizing their salvation. Need I remind us that as Christians we are in a life-and-death struggle, with Christ on one side pleading for our surrender to Him, and Satan on the other side, pulling us down to perdition? The enemy is quite aware of how attractive the critical and negative can be.

For example, offer people 10 pages of exposés of church problems and criticism of church policies and leadership. At the same time offer them 10 pages of soul-winning accounts, reports of progress in the church, or God's blessings in individual lives. Which will be read first, or read at all? The fallen mental chemistry of all of us seems to enjoy the former. We revel in juicy details of wrong and errors. Such may sell newspapers, but it will not build Christian character (see Phil. 4:8). How much we like to discuss the latest rumor, but how seldom do we find ourselves talking about our Saviour!

Spiritual sickness

Furthermore, I have learned that those who feed on criticism and are ever searching through the dirt and filth for errors and corruption in the church often fail to find true fulfillment in life themselves. Strangely, some try to build up their own egos by tearing something down. It is far easier to expose sin and evil than to expound on the cross of Christ.

Once we allow ourselves to travel through the valleys of vinegar, the sweetness and wholesomeness of what Jesus is doing in and through His church goes unnoticed. The mind sees what it is trained to dwell upon. Maliciousness, skepticism, and cynicism are diseases difficult to overcome.

I know this from personal experience. In my earlier years, I developed a rather critical attitude. I sadly confess that early in my ministry I thrived, at times, on the faults of church leaders. I remember a fiery letter I wrote to my old friend F. D. Nichol. His sweet reply disarmed me completely. (The point I was making was not necessarily wrong, but my attitude and spirit were!)

As years went by, I found myself feeding more and more on the church's problems. I didn't publicly criticize, but in my heart I found an estrangement with my brethren, which left me empty. My relationship with Jesus Christ became extremely fragile. Personal devotions were often interrupted by irritation over something I knew was happening in the church. The day came when I reached the conclusion that my own soul was at stake. I was building barriers between my own heart and my fellow workers and my God. Gradually, through the help of the Lord, I began to look for the good and to see the best. I still have a long way to go, but I thank God for the direction the Lord is leading me.

So I fear for the spiritual well-being of those whose work revolves around the negative.

Then, too, their production and organizations require cash to operate. The amount of money siphoned from the church by these "Adventist Amalekites" and their supporters would be enough, no doubt, to hold sizable yearly evangelistic crusades in major cities or to expand our radio-TV ministry. Every dollar diverted from the true mission of the church hinders the fulfillment of the commission God has given us.

My second concern is for our poor sheep who get hold of these documents and read them. Deep impressions are made on their minds. Questions are raised. Doubts are strengthened. Who is accountable, then, for souls that have been discouraged and misled? Who will eradicate the poison that has been taken in by the reader?

Think of what would happen if the tongues and pens of those turning out these negative productions would be used to the glory of God in speaking words of encouragement and confidence! I urge those with talents for speaking and writing to use these abilities to strengthen God's people and to encourage His leaders who are striving to advance the gospel. Let those who have a burden to set things straight go to their neighbors with the glorious news of Christ's plan to set straight sin-twisted lives. Let those who feel convicted that they must explore every facet of some church problem and expose it to those within and without the church begin to explore the fantastic truths in God's Word and set these before the people. Let those who rejoice in ferreting out some secret sin of the brethren study the secret and hidden things in the Word.

Stop sniping

I plead with "Adventist Amalekites" to stop this sniping at the heels of modern spiritual Israel. Rather, let us link arms together and in true Christian love work out our differences. Then we can join in the unity for which Jesus so eloquently prayed. One thing is certain. No one can truly pray the prayer of Christ in John 17 and at the same time undermine the church.

"But," says someone, "unity does not mean ignoring problems, hoping they will disappear. Unity does not mean saying all is well with the church, when all is *not* well."

I agree. Lest anyone feel I have assumed the ostrich posture, let me assure you that I am as aware as anyone that this church has problems that need to be acknowledged and solved. (In fact, I am probably more aware of these problems than are some who spend their time mimeographing, printing, and recording what they *do* know!) I am aware of the moral and ethical problems that may exist at times among both ministers and members in our church. But I do not believe that the solution to these things lies in sowing cynicism, criticism, castigation, innuendo, and suspicion by means of proliferating productions that spread these matters before all who will listen. I don't deny that the church has problems, although I also believe that she has more wholesome, positive, and uplifting aspects than her critics can imagine. I don't deny that we as leaders in the church have made mistakes and that in some cases we may have brought upon ourselves the criticisms that we are receiving. The unity Christ prayed for doesn't demand that we keep silent in the face of sin or error. But it does demand that we respond to such things as responsible members of Christ's body. There are proper ways for effecting changes and righting wrongs and getting the church back on track when she has lost her way.

The tragedy is to see such a prodigal squandering of precious brainpower and money in such negative pursuits when the church needs every bit of help possible in doing a constructive work in forwarding the banner of Prince Emmanuel throughout the world.

Chapter 16

A Letter to My God
on the Task Before Us

My dear heavenly Father:

As you know, the purpose of an "open" letter is to share thoughts not only with the One to whom the letter is addressed, but also with those who *ought* to read it. Of course, in Your case a letter isn't necessary at all. You know without my writing how I feel about the plan of One Thousand Days of Reaping.[1] You know, too, that I believe in and support the visible, organized body that we on earth call the Seventh-day Adventist Church. You've told us that it is the supreme earthly object of Your affection, and I'm confident that is true in spite of our failures to follow Your counsel explicitly. So even if I seem to be negative at times in this letter, You'll understand that I don't mean in any way to tear down the body that You love and that Your Son gave Himself to consecrate and cleanse so that it could be without stain or wrinkle or blemish. I'm sure some in the church, though, will be unhappy with certain things I write to You.

You're aware, of course, of last [1981] Annual Council's action. It's another attempt to give priority to evangelism, to put actual soul winning at the top of our agenda not only in every segment of our ministries but in our actual expenditures of money, time, and energies.

As You know, a number of our world divisions are making excellent membership gains, comparatively speaking. Some divisions seem to be in a holding pattern, it's true. But when I think about the energetic genesis of this church, back during the great Advent movement, and the way it has entered and established work in more countries and cultures than any other Protestant church, I can't help but dream of what could happen if we really took seriously the concepts contained in the "One Thousand Days of Reaping" document!

Soul winning—the only objective

But I can't help wondering also if this will be just another document that will eventually find a resting place in the archivists' tombs. Maybe You want it to go there! But if I correctly understand Your plan for this church, isn't soul winning (and soul nurturing, of course) the main objective (maybe the *only* objective) You have given us? To rescue souls from Satan's pit, to turn them from everlasting death to eternal life—isn't this why Your Son came as an infant to live with us? Isn't this why He spent some 30 years living an unselfish, perfect life and devoted the last three and a half years to training a few humble, unlearned men to preach the good news of the salvation He provided? Isn't this why He sealed His work with His own blood? After His resurrection, didn't Your Son return to heaven, where He works unceasingly in the heavenly sanctuary, His command center, for the purpose of salvaging lost humanity? Isn't it true, Father, that the salvation of a soul is the *only* event that causes all heaven to rejoice, while at the same time it stirs up a fierce intensity of hatred in Satan's heart?

Your Son, when He was here with us, told us clearly about Satan's attitude toward us. He said that the devil is not only a liar and the father of lies but a murderer from the beginning. And then You had Peter describe him as a lion bent on devouring people. Isn't this what the great controversy is all about?

I like the way Your Son summed up this controversy: "The thief comes only to steal and kill and destroy; I have come that they may have life and have it to the full" (John 10:10, NIV). The way He uses the word *only* to describe the thief's work makes it clear to my mind that we can have no compromise with the devil. And if I know anything at all about Your Son, He is just as determined to save people as the devil is to destroy them. It is a fight to the finish with no truce, no respite, no detente, and no bargaining.

Our first task

I believe You know the end from the beginning (although some of us are toying with the idea that You don't really know *everything* and are growing in Your knowledge even as we are supposed to grow). But I don't have Your total knowledge, so I have some questions regarding the church's response to "One Thousand Days of Reaping." Here we are in the midst of a mortal combat. I confess that it's difficult to put my finger on any denominational activity that could be classified as out-and-out evil. However, if the great controversy theme is what I think it is, and if the gospel commission means what it says, I can't help feeling that we are involved in some activities that aren't of primary importance. In fact, they are detrimental to the evangelistic thrust of the church.

For example, think of the way we are spending money, time, and energy to erect plush structures. (I'm sorry! I forgot for a moment that You are acquainted with all these things far better than I am and could give me examples I haven't even dreamed of.) But remember how one of the points in the 1976 Annual Council action, "Evangelism and Finishing God's Work," was the setting of limitations of building projects? One statement specifically stated, "Let us demonstrate to our people and to the world that we do not believe in building extravagantly, as though we intended to make this world our home. We must remember that the only things which will survive the destruction of the last days are the souls that are prepared for the coming of the Lord. . . . The one purpose of this economy would be to release more funds for the church to use in giving the last warning message to every nation, kindred, tongue, and people."

Since this action was taken, it seems to me that there have been dedications of church offices, institutions, and places of worship that could be categorized as extravagant and out of harmony with our professed priority on soul saving. And this expense is being incurred at a time when the world economy is anything but stable and seems to be careening toward a recession.

Practicing true stewardship

You're fully aware, too, how many of our sacrificing members have become disillusioned over excessive expenditures on brick, mortar, stone, and wood. Their hearts long to see the work finished and Your Son return. There is even discouragement among some congregations facing unnecessarily large monthly payments on building debts. We who preach stewardship principles to Your people in an attempt to train them in systematic benevolence dare not forget our own responsibilities as leaders to practice true stewardship principles in the use of these sacred funds so sacrificially given. Father, You have given us the wonderful concept of an owner-manager relationship to illustrate Your position and ours. Sometimes I think we who are leaders of Your church—Your ministers—have come to believe that *we* are both owners and managers and that the church members are merely to acquiesce in our management. Somehow remind us as leaders not to yield to the temptation to usurp Your place as Owner and abort Your stated mission for this church. The precious sheep You have entrusted to us as shepherds should be able to have confidence that the funds they give to this cause are being handled with great care and are being conserved for the purpose of extending the borders of Your kingdom through all forms of effective evangelism. If we could know, as You know, the exact day of Your Son's return, I'm sure there would be a revolution in our whole financial program. We would sacrifice and conserve funds as never before for the one purpose of reaching and saving lost humanity.

Focus on the value of a soul

There is something else regarding this reaping plan, Father. It is much more than a numerical emphasis; it's an attempt to focus our attention on the value of a soul. If we could only see through Your eyes the pricelessness of people! If we could only fathom the real reason Your Son became man. Why He came to live with us, walking amidst those whose goal was to destroy Him, and who finally did. Why He died on a cross. Why this incomparable Jesus condescended to visit our lost world. If we could only realize His real motivation! Surely He didn't do this for buildings or for organizational positions or for political reasons or for power and fame. His humiliating experience had only one purpose as far as we earthbound sinners are concerned: to rescue us from Satan's clutches. I know He went through this to vindicate You before the universe, but doesn't that very vindication consist in showing the universe that Your character of love couldn't rest easy until as many of Your estranged children as possible were reconciled, even if it meant the death of Jesus Himself?

This priority for soul winning has another reason, Father. It hopes to combine theology with evangelism. We spend enough time debating and discussing doctrinal points. It's a mystery to You, I'm sure, how some ministers and teachers can spend so much pulpit and classroom time playing ego-building games with parishioners and students who desperately need to have a saving knowledge of Christ both for themselves and to share with others. It's an amazement to us, so it certainly *must* be to You, that there are "Gibeonite Adventists" who can use their talents and time producing documents that subtly undermine the beliefs and mission of this church just as the mixed multitude weakened Israel on her march to Canaan. Oh, how much a radical change is needed in our thinking! A radical reordering of our priorities! If we truly mean business in making soul winning our first work, then drastic changes are necessary on every level of church organization.

Needed: radical changes

Your intent for us (if I read aright Your revelations regarding our lifestyle, goals, and objectives) is that church leaders free themselves, at any cost, from the numerous demands made upon their time and energy that do not really contribute to the salvation of souls. In this respect Your Son set us an example when asked to settle an inheritance dispute. He replied, "Man, who appointed me a judge or an arbiter between you?" (Luke 12:14, NIV).

To take seriously Your intent for us would mean a change in our educational and health-care systems. It would mean serious alterations in our training of ministers. On this point, Father, is there some way—a special revelation, a vision, an angel messenger, or whatever—that You could appeal to the leadership of this church to train ministers as Jesus trained them? For three and a half years the greatest Teacher the world has ever known trained His disciples for service by personal contact, association, and example. These original seminarians walked and talked with Him. They heard His words of cheer and encouragement to the weary and heavy laden. They saw the manifestation of His power on behalf of the sick and dying. In His classroom on the mountainside, or beside the sea, or walking through the fields, He revealed to them the mysteries of the kingdom of God. They traveled with Him from town to town and watched Him carefully unfold the truths of the way of salvation to despondent souls who had given up all hope. He could have revealed to them tremendous philosophies, concepts, and ideas. He could have inundated them with a barrage of knowledge, but He imparted to them only that which they could use in helping people to the kingdom. On every one of His journeys they could see how He talked to people, whether in crowded streets, lonely desert, by lakeside, or in the mountains. They shared His frugal fare and, with Him, were sometimes hungry and often weary.

What a revolution would take place in the church, Father, if we could train men with this on-the-job type of instruction! True, we have one small soul-winning institute in Chicago trying to combine both practical and theoretical training, but it is having a struggle. I might as well be honest with You, Father

(You know it as well as I do, anyway). Some among us are less than enthusiastic about the soul-winning institute. But the point is, Your Son sets us a tremendous example of where our priority should be.

A spiritual renewal

I must end this letter. I am planning to write You again in the future. But I must add just another thought or two. This "One Thousand Days of Reaping" plan has in its introduction a very important concept: the spiritual renewal of our lives as leaders. There can be no finishing of Your work, no priority given to evangelism, unless at the same time there is this spiritual renewal. Your Son promised that the Holy Spirit would be poured out in a special way on His followers. That took place initially and got the early church off to a tremendous start. The disciples were so filled with love for Your Son and for those for whom He died that the influence of the Spirit converted thousands as they preached and prayed. What rejoicing there must have been in the courts of heaven as Your followers, filled with the Holy Spirit, exhibited such love for one another and for lost humanity! Your Son's disciples, as executors of His will, brought the world the treasures of eternal life. They took literally the majestic missionary charter to go to the world with the gospel.

You have given to this church the same command in the framework of the three angels' messages. We are to preach that same gospel to every nation, kindred, tongue, and people. This means we are not to wait for the people to come to us, but we are to go to the people with Your glorious truth.

Finally, Father, I don't want to give the impression that I think we are able to go out and bring the final message of the gospel to the world apart from You and the Holy Spirit's power. No argument, however logical and irrefutable, will melt a heart or break through the hardness of worldliness and rebellion. Only the Holy Spirit can make our lips eloquent to save. Only a living knowledge of Your Son will make our witness effective. Every word and action is to fasten attention upon the all-powerful name of Your Son, Jesus Christ. He alone possesses that vital power by which sinners may be saved. His name is to be our watchword, our badge of distinction, our bond of union, our authority for our course of action, and the force of our success. We are to recognize nothing that does not bear His name.

It would be very dramatic and wonderful if today we could have the same thing happen to us that happened to the disciples when after Pentecost they determined to do everything possible to confess Your Son bravely before the world. Father, help us, if You can, to pray the same way they prayed during Pentecost. Help us to show the same intense earnestness for a fitness to meet men and women and to have the ability and sensitivity to speak words that will lead them to Christ. As I read about their early experience my heart cried out that Your Son would fit us with a special unction to do the work of soul saving.

We are so bogged down with details, plans, promotions, boards, projects, and committee meetings that we hardly have time even to have a burden for the salvation of souls! In addition, many of us are spending so much time on sports, TV, amusements, recreation, or running around the world seeing this and that that we are not really doing the work that You want us to do.

I hope that our "One Thousand Days of Reaping" will do something for this church to help us to focus on the work that You apparently consider more important than anything else—the saving of souls.

I appreciate this opportunity of writing to You. I want to thank You for all the correspondence You have sent me through the Scriptures and the pages of the Spirit of Prophecy. I can only praise Your name for Your goodness and Your power and say I hope that, along with my fellow ministers, I will respond in a positive way to Your appeal to go out, search for the lost, and bring them back to Your fold again.

Your unworthy and submissive servant,

Bob Spangler

[1] One Thousand Days of Reaping was the evangelistic plan of the world church from 1982-85, when 1,000 people were expected to be baptized every day.

Chapter 17

Pastoring: The Highest Calling

What's wrong with being a pastor? Nothing! In fact, it's great! Unfortunately, our system of church organization has not always assigned the pastor the place of foremost value and recognition. In fact, pastors have not always viewed themselves in the proper light. I don't believe for a moment that we have knowingly done this. But like the second law of thermodynamics, which tells us that time causes decay and disorganization, we have allowed time and events to erode the pastoral image from that of the highest calling God has given to something that is less than all-important.

At the same time, the importance of the individual member has eluded us as well. Let me illustrate: On an elevator in the General Conference building, I introduced myself to a stranger and asked his name. His immediate response was to remark timidly, "I am only a layman." I blurted back, "Brother, don't ever say you are *only* a layman! If it weren't for you, and others like you, we wouldn't have this elevator, much less this building."

I have heard similar responses from workers who when asked about their duties reply, "I am only a pastor!" This answer makes me feel sick, and I ask, "What has leadership done to create such an attitude on the part of those who are absolutely indispensable to our church?" Administrators, et cetera, may not be absolutely essential, but pastors and their congregations are!

What has caused this despicable system of false values? Why is it that we unconsciously question the success of ministers if after 40 years they retire from a pastorate without ever having done anything except be a pastor? Why is our usual attitude, "I wonder why they never succeeded?" Succeeded in what? "Well, I mean they never moved to departmental or administrative work. Evidently, they didn't have what it took to rise above a pastorate!"

Why can't we somehow place the proper valuation on the skills and dedication necessary to be a truly good, effective pastor? If we properly understood this matter, I am convinced our attitude would be something like this: "Yes, some have to settle for being administrators, departmental directors, teachers, editors, et cetera. These positions are necessary, and someone must fill them. Not everyone has the ability and calling to be a pastor; some must serve in less-demanding positions!"

The pastor and the church

Simple logic dictates that the existence and maintenance of a healthy church depend more upon the individual pastor than upon any other church employee, including the president of a division, union, local conference, or mission. The smallest, but most important, unit in our denominational system (aside from the individual member) is the church—the local congregation with its pastor. A church with its pastor can exist and function without presidents, secretaries, treasurers, departmental personnel, et cetera. But these individuals cannot exist apart from the local congregations.

This is *not* to say that any structure other than the local church is useless and unnecessary. On the contrary! The purpose of our organization is to bring strength to the churches. Furthermore, an organization such as ours can accomplish far more, in terms of a world outreach, than if each church were left on its own.

A strictly congregational form of church government has serious limitations. Had Seventh-day Adventists followed this plan, the scope of our world mission would have been seriously hampered. Small as we are numerically, we have a far-flung empire of churches, schools, hospitals, clinics, and institutions, made possible primarily because of our system. Without our God-given, unique organization, we would have a haphazard sprinkling of independent church units scattered here and there, united by fragile ties of impulse. Those few among us who are lobbying for congregationalism need to consider the consequences in terms of our ability to do anything really significant that demands the cooperation of our whole sisterhood of churches.

Still, the suprastructure of the church cannot exist without the support of the individual churches. What is a local conference? It is an organized group of churches with pastors within certain geographical boundaries. The union is simply an expansion of the territory, and so with the division—but the basic, irreducible element in our entire structure is the pastor and the local congregation. Eliminate the pastor and the local church, and our structure topples into oblivion. All, including myself, would be plunged into idleness, except pastors. (I fear some of us already are in a state of busy idleness.)

Jesus as pastor

When I consider the low estimate often placed on the pastorate, I wonder how we would have classified Jesus had He come to earth as a man in our day. No office, no secretary, no position, no title, no budget, no equipment. Someone has said, "He had no credentials but Himself." Could it be that our present-day Adventist system of values would categorize Jesus as a total failure? After all, here was a Man who was always saying or doing something to cause problems. He did not identify Himself with the people who were influential in the church, but of all things associated with thieves, whores, lepers, and the disabled. He even conversed and ate with those who were detested because of their racial background. When all is said and done, this Jesus can be classified only as an itinerant pastor—a circuit rider without a horse. Palestine was His territory. He worked hard as a shepherd of souls for several years before being killed. The strange thing about it all is that He aspired to no higher position than being a pastor—even unto death. No doubt Peter had in mind the Saviour's example in pastoral work when he wrote, "Feed the flock of God which is among you, taking the oversight thereof, not by constraint, but willingly . . . neither as being lords over God's heritage, but being ensamples to the flock. And when the chief Shepherd shall appear, ye shall receive a crown of glory that fadeth not away" (1 Peter 5:2-4).

Certainly, Christ's work falls in a pastoral category more than anything else. True, He was the chief administrator of the 12, but He led these men in a far different way than people are being led today. I do not mean to be critical, and perhaps it is impossible to perform our function as administrators in any other way. But Christ constantly led people by showing them personally how to seek, save, nurture, and uplift precious souls. He never sat down and wrote letters of instruction to the disciples; He gave them on-the-job training.

Neither did Christ follow the role of a departmental leader. We have no record of His sending out bulletins on various phases of the work. He never projected statistical goals or printed comparison lists to show where each disciple stood in terms of performance. Jesus was a Shepherd. He had a true pastor's heart. He was concerned over the welfare of the sheep, and He conveyed that concern to His associates who learned so well at His feet, at His side, in the marketplace, in the homes, on the hillside. Wherever Jesus went was a training center. He was a seminary on legs. He carried the library with Him in trees and sky, bird and animal, and, of course, the Scriptures.

Pastoring is not easy

Could it be that specialization has become so attractive to us because we desire to escape the heavy responsibility of being a pastor? Pastoring is not easy, especially today, with so many complex problems to deal with—divorce, adultery, abortion, drugs, rebellion, and a spirit of independence. Pastoring is a hard and hazardous duty. It demands courage and challenges the very best in the minister. Paul worked tirelessly as a soul-winning pastor. At the same time he was a persuasive orator, a matchless theologian, and met every hazard possible, including his final one—execution. Yet he was ever a pastor, with "the care of all the churches" on his shoulders. He was a true pattern for today's pastors.

It might seem easier to join the ranks of the administrators, but, believe me, faithful administrators today do not walk a smooth, rose-strewn patch of ease! Too often they are the punching bag for the rebellious and the insolent.

Then there is departmental work, and in a sense it *is* easier than being in the pastorate. Departmental leaders can skip and bound over the field, leaving church problems behind for the pastor to worry about. But they pay a price for this type of activity. Usually they form no long-lasting relationships. They live like people without a country. I know whereof I speak, for I sense my own need of staying with a group on a long-term basis, where I can form deep relationships.

Another problem departmental leaders face is that it can be much more difficult to maintain mental and even spiritual growth in such a situation than it is in a pastorate where one is forced to feed the sheep a well-balanced diet on a weekly basis over a long period of time. Departmental persons can get away with a few sermons a year since their congregations change every Sabbath. So if you are a pastor looking for greener pastures instead of staying with the sheep on a permanent basis, be careful lest you end up in a rather lonely desert of isolation.

Why, then, do we count it such a horrendous calamity if a person in an elected position becomes a church pastor again, either by choice or by not being reelected when the constituency feels that a change is needed? How often I have heard of nominating committees that were loath to replace a particular leader because no other elected position was available, and it was quite unthinkable for that person to lose face and become a pastor again. This was regarded as a step down. Interestingly enough, the individual who had to "step down" to the pastorate was probably proclaiming a few days earlier how important and sacred the work of the pastor is! Nothing equaled in meaning and significance the exalted position of the pastor *until* the speaker "stepped down" to the pastorate. How I wish this situation did not exist. But I would be less than honest if I tried to deny it.

One of the results of our failure as a church to build the pastor and help him sense the importance of his work is the lack of strong people in pastoral positions. This is not to say that we do not have strong pastors, but frankly there is a shortage of them. Too many times I have been called to recommend someone to fill the pulpit of a large church. Sometimes these larger churches are open for months at a time before a strong, organized, powerfully preaching, soul-winning pastor can be found. Could it be that we have allowed some of our strongest persons to go into other types of work? Important as these may be, nothing is as important as shepherding the sheep.

Toward a better pastoral image

We cannot deny the fact that we do need qualified leadership for administrative posts, but can't we do something that will create a better image of the pastor? I think we can. I am going to list only a few items, but there are other points one can think of that will help enhance the position and ministry of a faithful pastor in the eyes of the church and her members.

1. Wage scale imbalances. Our wage-scale system has a rather subtle, insidious status symbolism in it. Sometimes committees labor long and loud to increase the remuneration package of a particular job by one or two points to show its importance. The small amounts involved in these additional points indicate that it surely cannot be the money that is the major factor, but rather it is the status that is involved. A quick look at the wage scale indicates that there are literally dozens of positions in this church that exceed in pay what the top ordained pastor can reach. I believe that a qualified pastor should be able to reach the highest wage level this church offers ordained minsters. If this means wage parity, so let it be.

2. Greater representation on committees and boards. Let the pastor's voice be heard. Let them know that they have a brain to think and a mind to conceive ideas that may bring solutions to the problems we face. After all, people in the field should have a grasp of the reality of life and should be the best judge of any program conceived by those in the office.

3. Pastoral budgets to be cut last. When financial reverses come to a conference, do not swing the ax of budget reductions at pastoral budgets first, but eliminate office jobs before eliminating a pastor's job. Let the pastoral budgets be the last to be cut.

4. Give priority to the pastor's work. Put into practice the various elements that relate to pastors and their work as listed in "The Finishing of the Work" document voted at the 1976 Annual Council. These include clarifying the role of pastors and freeing them from peripheral matters so that they can concentrate on their major duties of spiritual nurture and evangelism.

Finally, a word to pastors. The church does not always demonstrate practically the high regard she professes for the pastors and their sacred work. Yet, you know, as no others can, that the delights and rewards of the parish pastor are truly unequaled. May God help you to look upon your work as the work that is most similar to that performed by Jesus Himself. Carry out your work in such a way that if you could borrow another life to spend again, you would spend it ministering in the pastorate.

Chapter 18

Can a God-Called Preacher Fail?

"Why did such a talented man as Jim leave the ministry and go into business?" "What happened to our pastor? How could he leave his wife for another woman?" "What's wrong with Preacher Bill? His attitude toward his work as a minister is so negative." "Why does our district leader act so discouraged all the time?"

The list can be endless. One could tally all the reasons for discouragement and depression among preachers. We could form committees by the dozen to ponder the problems leading to failure in ministry. Research organizations could be hired to analyze these problems and offer solutions. But isn't there at least one major factor that invariably enters any picture of failure among ministers?

Valid failures

Let us assume that the above examples of failure are persons who were qualified in every respect to be ministers of the gospel. There are some, both in and out of the ministry today, who are failures simply because we depend on human judgment alone in our selection of those to be ordained. Those who have not been called by God to the ministry and have failed are valid failures!

Ellen White "was shown that quite a number who were thinking it their duty to teach the word of God publicly had mistaken their work. They had no call to devote themselves to this solemn, responsible work. They were not qualified for the work of the ministry, for they could not instruct others properly."[1] She further stated that "God has repeatedly shown that persons should not be encouraged into the field without unmistakable evidence that He has called them. The Lord will not entrust the burden for his flock to unqualified individuals."[2]

When God calls a person to the ministry and the leaders are aware of it, that person can count on triumph in the work. There is no such thing as failure as long as that person follows the formula for success. God has never called anyone to failure, and that includes Noah! This does not mean to say that a God-called, thoroughly converted minister will never make a mistake nor experience at times what may appear as failure in the work.

As the world's Redeemer, Christ was constantly confronted with apparent failure. He, the messenger of mercy to our world, seemed to do little of the work He longed to do in uplifting and saving. Satanic influences were constantly working to oppose His way. But He would not be discouraged.[3]

Why Peter failed

Do you remember Peter's cursing denial of Christ? Peter was called and ordained by Christ, yet the divine commentary states that "Peter had prepared the way for his great sin."[4] What a thought! Imagine a person consciously or unconsciously preparing the way for failure. None think it strange to prepare for success, but few consider the concept of preparing for failure. Some may think that Peter's denial experience was most uncommon. Yet he followed the same pattern that every last one of us follows who fails. In my thinking, there are no exceptions. Just how did Peter prepare for failure? Speculation is unnecessary. The facts are that "it was in sleeping when Jesus bade him watch and pray that Peter had prepared the way for his great sin."[5]

It is well to remember that preparing for failure can involve more than one type of sleep. Physical unconsciousness is not the only way to induce insensitivity of mind, body, and soul. Those elements under our control that adversely affect any of our senses can be categorized as "sleep." Furthermore, anything, regardless of how honorable and right it is, that is permitted to come between us and our daily hours of study and prayer induces spiritual sleepiness. We are urged to "guard jealously your hours for prayer, Bible study, and self-examination. Set aside a portion of each day for a study of the Scriptures and communion with God. Thus you will obtain spiritual strength, and will grow in favor with God."[6]

Empty pulpits

How many Adventist pulpits would be vacant next Sabbath if ministers were not allowed to preach unless they had spent 12 hours (two hours a day) in Bible study and three hours (30 minutes a day) in prayer during the preceding week? A rather solemn conjecture?

Modern preachers live in an intense environment. The world with its post offices, bookstands, newspapers, billboards, and airwaves floods our eyes and ears with materials both good and bad. Even the church cranks out an amazing amount of wonderful propaganda that could claim a major portion of our reading and thinking time if we let it. No person can encompass even a small part of this deluge of materials, which in the main is putting humankind to sleep.

How should ministers relate themselves to this problem? The same way Peter should have related himself to his situation in the garden. "Had those hours in the garden been spent in watching and prayer, Peter would not have been left to depend upon his own feeble strength. He would not have denied his Lord."[7]

How desperately our church needs men and women of prayer and study.

Spiritual digitalis

The digitalis for spiritual heart failure among ministers is a daily dose of knee bending and Bible study. We can build churches, organize campaigns, be pastors of the century, sit on a score of committees, travel to and fro throughout the earth, but when we refuse to take time for prayer and Bible study each day—I repeat, each day, not tomorrow, not next month, not next year, but each day—we have failed! Some reason that when a certain project is finished they will do differently, but that time usually never comes. Furthermore, when one fails to spend time with God on any particular day, that failure is one that cannot be rectified. Time cannot be recalled. It is gone forever! A second chance to make that day go right will never be given.

Sit down, my fellow minister, and count the days when you did not spend time with God. Certainly, most of us accomplish something from the standpoint of church work. We make some visits, preach a sermon or two, write letters, but this is merely sharing ourselves—the giving of ourselves in service. What I am talking about it not giving of ourselves. I am talking about receiving from God for ourselves those spiritually nutritious elements that make it possible for us to give properly of ourselves to others.

Furthermore, I am not advocating a cloistered life of study and prayer totally disconnected from service. Never! The two go hand in hand. My fear is that many Adventist ministers do not take time, for whatever reason, to let God mold the soul, to strengthen convictions, and bring vitality and life to the spiritual nature that results from communion with Him.

A lesson from the falcon

Come with me to a football stadium. Thousands are jammed in to see the U.S. Air Force Academy play. Just before the game begins, a sleek free-flight falcon is released. It gracefully soars upward over the stadium. Finally the bird circles, beating the air with its tapered wings, and waits for the signal. The crowd is as silent as just before a crucial play. Suddenly the bird folds its wings and drops like a jet airplane on a strafing run. Its zoom-lens eyes keep in focus a fist-sized leaders lure whirling on a string above the head of its trainer and master, who is known as a falconer. At the last split second, it brakes from 175 miles per hour to zero, sinks its talons in the lure, and rides it to the ground.

The training program of these symbolic airborne mascots of the Air Force Academy yields important lessons for us. Handlers must spend three to five hours every day with their birds. In good weather the birds are flown for about half an hour. When the weather is too bad for flying, the trainers take care of other duties, but there is one duty that must be performed without fail. The handler must hold the falcon each day even if the weather is too poor for flying. The smallest break in this routine undermines the trust between handler and bird, and undoes months of work.

We, as wild birds with spirits that need to be tamed; we who are prone to fly away from our Master; we who by nature are sinful and uncontrollable; we who are rebellious and cantankerous; we who permit anything and everything, including good things such as church work, to keep us under pressure so that we are depressed and discouraged; we who feel that we cannot take time for God as we should—oh, how desperately we need a daily handling by our divine Falconer, Jesus Christ!

Why not prepare for success instead of failure by beginning this day to spend time with God on an organized, routine basis? If this plan is earnestly and sincerely followed, there is no reason for failure in the Christian ministry!

---

1   *Testimonies,* vol. 2, p. 553.

2   *Ibid.,* vol. 1, p. 209.

3   See *The Desire of Ages,* p. 678.

4   *Ibid.,* p. 713.

5   *Ibid.*

6   *Gospel Workers,* p. 100.

7   *The Desire of Ages,* p. 714.

Chapter 19

Counsels on Counseling

We ministers are often faced with the need to counsel. In our attempts to help people solve their problems, we face certain pitfalls as counselors. Our calling as undershepherds does not guarantee immunity to falling into these traps. The casualty list is growing longer with the inevitable ugly scars being left on both ministers and members. Since everybody loses in these wrong types of counseling sessions, the ministry of this church should continually refresh their minds as to God's plan for helping people. If His instruction is sought and heeded, the church will be spared from an enormous amount of heartbreak and disillusionment.

Jesus plainly told His disciples that He was sending them "out as sheep in the midst of wolves" (Matt. 10:16, RSV). In this rebellious world of ours there are far more wolves than there are sheep. In fact, everybody is born a wolf and stays a wolf unless the new birth transforms them into sheep. So we have murderous, cheating, lying, thieving, lustful wolves roaming our planet. Many of these wolves have deep desires to do what is right but they are morally frail. This type of wolf can be more dangerous than the obviously vicious ones.

There are some wolves who haven't the slightest idea they are wolves. They feel certain they are sheep. Occasionally when they smile before a mirror one of their fangs may partially show, but memory is short and eyes see what they want to see, so they merrily go their way thinking they are sheep.

Special temptations

Picture a preacher who should be a sheep himself trying to handle these wolves as they come to him for help. Even the strongest of us is constantly in danger, especially in certain types of counseling situations. Regardless of how good a sheep we may be, we have the warning that "Satan's special temptations are directed against the ministry. He knows that ministers are but human, possessing no grace or holiness of their own; that the treasures of the gospel have been placed in earthen vessels, which divine power alone can make vessels unto honor. He knows that God has ordained ministers to be a powerful means for the salvation of souls, and that they can be successful in their work only as they allow the eternal Father to rule their lives. Therefore he tries with all his ingenuity to lead them into sin, knowing that their office makes sin in them more exceeding sinful; for in committing sin, they make themselves ministers of evil."[1]

Let's alter the picture a bit. What if the preacher is a wolf in sheep's clothing, and another wolf comes to see him? All too often the carnal natures of both wolves cause a problem, especially if the wolf seeking help is an attractive female with a problem related to sex. Or worse still, what if a needy sheep comes to a wolf-type minister? This is putting it bluntly, but the agonizing problems that so often result from non-Christian techniques of counseling warrant stating the case plainly. It is our desire especially to spare our younger ministers the trauma of moral shipwreck. Certain basic rules must be adhered to for safety's sake by our workers, no matter what their age.

Obviously, the minister needs to be a converted person. This is the first prerequisite of a Christian counselor. This truth is inherent in Jesus' warning that we are sheep in the midst of wolves.

Christ added a second qualification. "Be wise as serpents and innocent as doves" (Matt. 10:16, RSV). The serpent, the accepted emblem of wisdom, is a wary, sharp-sighted creature. It seems to have an innate ability to sense danger and the skill to quietly glide away from it. Combine these qualities with the dove-like elements of simplicity and harmlessness, and you have a sensible formula for genuine goodness. Our hearts need to cry out to God continuously for help to make us perceptive as serpents and guileless as doves!

Christ's serpent-dove analogy is so applicable in the minister's dealing with those of the opposite sex. It is my conviction that all minister-counselors, trained or untrained, degreed or nondegreed, should follow carefully the advice given to a conference president by Ellen White:

"If any woman, no matter who, casts herself upon your sympathy, are you to take her up and encourage her and receive letters from her and feel a special responsibility to help her? My brother, you should change your course with regard to such matters, and set a right example before your brother ministers. Keep your sympathy for the members of your own family, who need all that you can give them. When a woman is in trouble, let her take her trouble to women. If this woman who has come to you has cause of complaint against her husband, she should take her trouble to some other woman who can, if necessary, talk with you in regard to it, without any appearance of evil. You do not seem to realize that your course in this matter is exerting a wrong influence. Be guarded in your words and actions."[2]

Send women to women

Note God's recommendation that we send maritally troubled women to other women. Even here, however, one must make certain that the woman to whom we send them for help is stable and spiritually mature. What a wonderful blessing it is when a minister has a consecrated, knowledgeable wife who can help the women members with their intimate problems.

The above admonition may seem Victorian, but it is more valid today than ever before. We live in a raw, open society. Chatter about sex and sex problems is about as common and frequent as radio-TV weather forecasts. Whether it be among the sophisticated or the subcultured, negative attitudes toward sexual promiscuity and perversions are in the minority. Our society is no longer living in the middle of a sexual revolution. The revolution is all but over, and the sexually promiscuous and perverted have pretty well won the battle. I am appalled at some of the so-called Christian literature dealing with marriage and sex relations that is currently coming off the presses. It is a strange, vile mixture of purity and rottenness. In the midst of this sex cesspool it is particularly mandatory for us as ministers to be as careful as possible in our counseling procedures.

Counseling guidelines

In view of the rapidly deteriorating moral standards that characterize our society, the following guidelines for ministers who must counsel the women members of their flocks should be carefully considered and practiced.

1. Have someone such as your wife or local elder with you when calling on the women members of your congregation who are likely to be alone.
2. When counseling a woman in your church office, leave the door ajar.
3. Always refuse to meet a woman who desires counseling under clandestine circumstances. Isolated locations or the automobile are extremely poor places for such counseling.
4. If a woman "manifests undue affection and mourns that her husband does not love her and sympathize with her, do not try to supply this lack. Your only safe and wise course in such a case is to keep your sympathy to yourself. Such cases are numerous. Point such souls to the Burden Bearer, the true and safe Counselor."[3]
5. Keep your hands off the opposite sex. A pat on the back or a squeeze of the arm, innocent though your intentions may be, has more than once started a disastrous chain of events.
6. Watch your words carefully. Frivolous conversation, seemingly innocent at first, can lead to problems later. Joking usually breaks down appropriate barriers.
7. Never encourage individuals to go into detail regarding some sinful episode they have experienced. Rather, use tact in discouraging those who are anxious to divulge everything.
8. "Rebuke the woman who will praise your smartness, holding your hand as long as she can retain it in her own. Have little to say to persons of this class; for they are the agents of Satan, and carry out his plans by laying bewitching snares to beguile you from the path of holiness."[4]
9. Never divulge any of your failings, secrets, or the intimate personal details of your own marriage relationship.
10. Direct women with sexual problems to your wife or some competent woman counselor whom you know to be spiritually sound.

Although the above guidelines may seem to be archaic nonsense to some, the example set for us 2,000 years ago cannot be improved on. "He manifested consistency without obstinacy, benevolence without weakness, tenderness and sympathy without sentimentalism. He was highly social; yet He possessed a reserved dignity that did not encourage undue familiarity."[5]

1   *Gospel Workers*, p. 124.
2   *Evangelism*, pp. 460, 461.
3   *Testimonies*, vol. 5, p. 598.
4   *Evangelism*, p. 679.
5   *Ibid.*, p. 636.

Chapter 20

Rx for Spiritual Dullness

"How is it, . . . that this untrained man has such learning?" (John 7:15, NEB). This question obviously did not imply that Christ was illiterate, but rather that He had no formal theological training. Even as a 12-year-old child He astounded the church's best minds with His questions and answers. The deep truths He skillfully brought to the surface by His innocent questions intrigued His erudite audience. "All that heard him were astonished at his understanding and answers" (Luke 2:47).

Christ did not enter our world with a head and heart filled with knowledge and wisdom. In assuming the garb of humanity His spiritual, mental, physical, and social powers expanded by His conformity and obedience to those principles that govern all human development (see Luke 2:52). When tempted by Satan in the wilderness, Jesus responded, "It is written, That man shall not live by bread alone, but by every word of God" (Luke 4:4). These same words had been given by Christ through Moses to the children of Israel nearly 15 centuries before (see Deut. 8:3). It is an unchangeable, eternal principle that proper study of Scriptures will result in spiritual growth. In fact, this is the only certain way to spiritual growth.

Opinions of men, deductions of science, and declarations of ecclesiastical councils must be subject to a plain "thus saith the Lord." Jesus learned the Scriptures from childhood. He understood that the Bible is our only safeguard against error and delusion. Note Christ's reply to the wily Sadducees who tried to trip Him on a sticky theological question: "You are mistaken, and surely this is the reason: you do not know either the scriptures or the power of God" (Mark 12:24, NEB).

One day Jesus joined a gloomy pair of His followers on the road to Emmaus. He listened to their discussion, which centered on the crucifixion. After some time Jesus interrupted to ask why they were talking the way they were. Cleopas turned and perhaps tearfully asked, "Are you the only person staying in Jerusalem not to know what has happened there in the last few days?" (Luke 24:18, NEB).

These believers should have been aware of the clear teaching of the Scriptures. Hadn't they listened months before as Jesus plainly explained what the prophets had to say about His death, burial, and resurrection? Now their minds were confused because they did not clearly sense the import of what Jesus had said. Emotions and feelings ruled their thoughts, preventing them from grasping that which would have been so comforting to them in their bitter disappointment.

The Saviour longed to help them in their distress. Yet He chose *not* to do what most of us would have done. Rather than open their eyes at this point He seemingly added to their discomfort by chiding, "How dull you are!" He hastened to show them what He meant: "How slow to believe all that the prophets said!" There followed a thorough study of Old Testament prophecies: "He began with Moses and all the passages which referred to himself in every part of the scriptures."

Note that Jesus did not perform a miracle. He did not philosophize or psychologize. Nor did He quote the writings of others outside the Scriptures. Rather He riveted their minds on the words by which a person must live. He showed that the Scriptures, not their feelings and senses, were the strongest foundation for their faith and mental stability. Here was the only remedy for their depressing dullness.

What was the result? When their eyes were finally opened and they joyously rushed back over those seven miles to Jerusalem, they exclaimed, "Did we not feel our hearts on fire as he talked with us on the road and explained the scriptures to us?" (verse 32, NEB). When did their hearts glow with the warmth of understanding and love? *Before* their eyes were opened! When the Word was expounded, then came this thrilling experience. It is a simple but profound truth that lives are touched and changed through the preaching of the Word.

Christ's regard for the truth revealed in the Old Testament is summed up in Luke 16:31: "If they hear not Moses and the prophets, neither will they be persuaded, though one rose from dead." Need it be pointed out how multitudes today would choose as a basis for their faith some miracle or ecstatic experience rather than the simple, plain "It is written"?

In these last days great delusions are certain to come. The antichrist will perform marvelous works in our sight. Multitudes will be swept off their feet. Truth will be so closely counterfeited by error that the only possibility of delineating between the two will be through the microscope of Scripture. Bible testimony must test every concept and miracle. How earnestly we as ministers should fortify our own minds and the minds of our parishioners with the written Word. If we are to interest our members in the Scriptures we must first demonstrate a real interest in and love for the study of the Scriptures ourselves. If our hearts are on fire with the Word our people will recognize it and long for a similar experience.

A word of caution. It is totally insufficient merely to keep abreast with what others have to say about the Bible. Preachers who attempt to keep up with the religious concepts and interpretations of Scripture pouring from publishing houses today will probably have little or no time to study the Book for themselves. This is not intended to be wholesale condemnation of all religious books outside the Bible. But it is an appeal for sharp discernment and discrimination in what we read, in order to be able to spend more of our energy and time in Bible study.

The authoritative, infallible revelation of God must be our source of power, our standard of right and wrong. Certainly the mind, fickle as it is, cannot know the right way unless controlled by biblical principles. To avoid spiritual dullness and to gain a living experience with the Lord, we leaders of the flock must spend several hours each day in intensive study of the Word.

Chapter 21

The Power of Witnessing

One night Zechariah was awakened out of his sleep by an angel. The angel portrayed before him a rather interesting combination of golden candlesticks, a bowl, lamps, olive trees, and pipes. Casual readers of the fourth chapter of Zechariah might consider this a Rube Goldberg device, but the spiritually-minded can discover great significance in Zechariah's description of what he was shown.

I picture two olive trees from which two pipes lead to a beautiful golden bowl, which sits on top of a rather large branched candlestick. From the bowl seven separate pipes branch out to the arms of the candlestick that supports seven lamps. The golden oil flows through the two pipes into the bowl and continues through the seven pipes to the seven lamps. This oil is not the kind of oil we know of but a special kind of oil called in the Scriptures "golden oil."

When Zechariah saw all of this elaborate equipment with the oil running through it he asked the angel, What does all of this mean? The angel's reply is most significant. "This is the word of the Lord . . . saying, Not by might, nor by power, but by my spirit, saith the Lord of hosts" (Zech. 4:6).

The two olive trees are the holy ones that stand in God's presence. From these the Holy Spirit is imparted to certain human beings on earth, human instrumentalities who are totally committed and consecrated to His service. The golden oil of the Holy Spirit imparts light and power to God's instrument, which in turn imparts light and love to others. There is a question which faces all of us today: Can we impart that which we ourselves have not received? Can an unlit candle produce light that will pierce the darkness?

Christ lived the truth

Two men were walking from Jerusalem to a little village called Emmaus. It was quite a walk—about seven miles. Their journey took place shortly after the resurrection of their Master, Jesus. You remember how the Master turned the twosome into a threesome and they began to talk about recent events relative to the crucifixion. It is interesting to note that Roman politics, the then current economic situation, the overcrowded conditions in Jerusalem, the devaluation of the shekel, the high prices of food, the need of salary increases, or even the weather had no place in their thoughts or discussion. One thing monopolized their conversation: the trial and crucifixion of Jesus, who to them "was a prophet mighty in deed and word before God and all the people" (Luke 24:19).

After they had expressed their deep disappointment over Christ's death and His seeming failure to redeem Israel, the Master began talking. His first words were "O fools," or as the *New English Bible* says, "How dull you are." Then He took the writings of Moses and expounded the prophecies, pointing out the fulfillment of them in His own life, death and resurrection. Christ's prophetic dissertation was so powerful, so convincing, so persuasive, that in later conversation these two disheartened disciples testified eloquently to each other in these words: "Did we not feel our hearts on fire as he talked with us on the road and explained the scriptures to us?" (Luke 24:32, NEB). That fire was seen in their subsequent action. They jumped up from the supper table that "same hour" and rushed seven miles back to Jerusalem to give their testimony to the other disciples. A fourteen-mile hike in one day is no small feat. Seven of those miles were walked in dejection; seven in rejoicing.

Suppose Caiaphas was the one doing the expounding on this journey. Let's assume that he spoke the same words and used the same prophecies that Jesus used. Let us also assume that he interpreted these prophecies exactly as Christ did. Let us assume that he brought these men to exactly the same conclusion that Jesus brought them to—that Christ indeed was the Messiah. Furthermore, let's assume that Caiaphas had no change of attitude and mind toward Christ while he was giving this Bible study, but he did it, and he did it well, because he was paid to do it. If this had been the case, do you think these men's hearts would have caught on fire? Would they have rushed back to Jerusalem with the good news of the resurrection?

If our answer is Yes, then is it really necessary to have the golden oil in order to communicate the gospel? "Christ taught the truth because He was the truth. His own thought, His character, His life experience, were embodied in His teaching. So with His servants: those who would teach the word are to make it their own by a personal experience. They must know what it is to have Christ made unto them wisdom and righteousness and sanctification and redemption. . . . Every minister of Christ's should be able to say with the beloved John, 'The life was manifested, and we have seen it, and bear witness, and show unto you that eternal life which was with the Father, and was manifested unto us.' 1 John 1:2."[1]

Does character have any effect?

Again, how far should we carry this point? Presumably most of us agree with this statement, but how important is it to us to be the truth? Often I ask myself, What kind of communicator am I? When I speak publicly or privately, is the seed that I sow mine? When I speak, is there a life of consistent Christianity behind my words? If not, can the seed sown spring up and grow properly? Or does the seed sown by an unconverted sower fall only on stony or thorny or wayside soil? What do *you* think?

Does the character of the preacher have any effect on his listeners as to their response to the words they are hearing? Please understand that I am not trying to be mystical in my thinking. God forbid. But over the years I have given much thought to this point. I have often wondered if there is a quality in the spoken or written word originating from consecrated sources that is not in the spoken or written word originating from unconsecrated sources. Does God bless in a special way, but not necessarily with outward show, the work done by a consecrated person—work that will stand for eternity?

During my college years I made friends with a certain young minister who confidentially told me one day that he was not living right. He went on to explain in detail some of his practices that gave unmistakable evidence that he was not a converted man. He admitted it, so I am not judging the man, merely giving his own testimony. He was holding meetings at the time of this conversation, and people were being baptized. Then he said, "God works in spite of the instrument." That started me thinking. Does God really work this way? Is this a fairly common occurrence? Does the work accomplished by self-confessed evildoers and charlatans have only temporary and not eternal results? Perhaps a work that may result in fattening our statistics and make good reports in our union papers will pass away in the end. If we say that eternal good may be accomplished by workers who lack the golden oil, then what does Ellen White mean when she says, "Only the work accomplished with much prayer, and sanctified by the merit of Christ, will in the end prove to have been efficient for good"?[2]

Or consider this statement: "It is God alone who can give success either in preparing or in circulating our publications. . . . Humble, fervent prayer will do more to promote the circulation of our books than will all the expensive ornamentation in the world. God has great and grand resources for man to lay hold of, and in the most simple manner will be developed the working of the divine agencies. The divine Teacher says: 'My Spirit alone is competent to teach and to convict of sin. Externals make only a temporary impression upon the mind. I will enforce truth on the conscience, and men shall be My witnesses, throughout the world asserting My claims on man's time, his money, his intellect.'"[3]

Can God use any kind of person?

The question is, Can God use any kind of person to teach His truth? Can God use any kind of person to write His literature? Can God use any kind of person to witness for His love? Can a sacred work be performed by secular persons? If we answer Yes, I ask again, Is it really necessary to have the golden oil to communicate the gospel?

How can we bring people face to face, mind to mind, heart to heart, with Christ unless we are possessed by the Holy Spirit? How can an evil individual speak good things that will really make an eternal impact on others?

Gehazi, the servant of Elisha, although associated with a man of God, apparently had not surrendered his life to the heavenly powers. You will recall he ended up a leper and probably died with this dread disease. It came upon him as a curse. His selfishness and greed for money got the best of him. One time Elisha responded to the urgent pleas of the Shunamite woman whose son had died. Elisha sent Gehazi with his staff to this poor woman's home and gave him specific instructions not to speak to anyone on his journey. He told Gehazi to place his staff "upon the face of the child" (2 Kings 4:31). Gehazi followed

Elisha's formula down to the last detail, but nothing happened. The Scriptures say that "there was neither voice, nor hearing" after Gehazi put the staff on his face. Is there a lesson in this for us? Elisha had the golden oil, poor Gehazi didn't. Isn't it the Person and the Power behind the individual who holds the staff that counts?

This is true even in musical presentations. The Lord gave us this counsel years ago. "In the meetings that are held, they are not to depend on worldly singers and theatrical displays to awaken an interest. How can those who have no interest in the Word of God, who have never read His word with a sincere desire to understand its truths, be expected to sing with the spirit and the understanding? How can their hearts be in harmony with the words of sacred song? How can the heavenly choir join in music that is only a form?"[4]

Even in the field of instrumental music, does the music played by converted individuals have a spiritual quality that is nonexistent in the music played by unconverted individuals? We are told, "Display is not religion nor sanctification. There is nothing more offensive in God's sight than a display of instrumental music when those taking part are not consecrated, are not making melody in their hearts to the Lord. The offering most sweet and acceptable in God's sight is a heart made humble by self-denial, by lifting the cross and following Jesus."[5]

During an Annual Council several years ago, a young college woman walked out on the platform and sat down beside a harp. Before she finished playing, the majority in that audience were gripped by the spirituality of the performance. The music was simple. Nothing overpowering or spectacular, but some way, somehow, the Spirit of God spoke through that girl and harp. I later found out who the girl was, and the testimony of those who knew her confirmed that she was a tremendous Christian and a wonderful influence in the school. Undoubtedly a person through whose life the golden oil flowed.

What about money?

I have wondered about money being wasted in our church. One day the thought struck me that any money secured or given by right motivation is never wasted. The widow's mite motivation ensures the money will be spent properly. If any money is wasted, it is only that money which is secured and given through wrong methods and motivations. Interesting thought, isn't it? In at least one instance Ellen White pointed out that some money given to the church has a curse on it. Speaking of donations received from those trafficking in liquor she said, "This very man may make large donations to the church; but will God accept of the money that is wrung from the family of the drunkard? It is stained with the blood of souls, and the curse of God is upon it. God says, 'For I the Lord love judgment, I hate robbery for burnt offering.'"[6]

From what has been said so far, I wouldn't be surprised if you were laboring under the impression that I think that any sermon, Bible study, radio program, special music, script, book, or whatever, produced or communicated by unconverted "servants of God," cannot possibly have any effect on individuals. Such is not the case. Jesus said He would use rocks as preachers if necessary. "A man may hear and acknowledge the whole truth, and yet know nothing of personal piety and true experimental religion. He may explain the way of salvation to others, and yet himself be a castaway. The truth is holy and powerful, and searches the intents and purposes of the heart. The importance and authority of the truth in the great plan of salvation originated in the divine Author, and are not rendered void or worthless because the instruments employed in their administration are unholy or unfaithful."[7]

But I firmly believe that if every worker in this church, whether he or she be janitor, typesetter, president, evangelist, nurse, doctor, pastor, or layperson, made it his or her first work to receive constantly fresh supplies of the golden oil and then went to work using sanctified brain cells and energy in thought and action to reach the world with the glorious gospel, we would see the might of the omnipotent God working in our behalf as we have never yet seen it. The church militant would be the church triumphant in a very short time.

What is success?

Often we ask, What is success? Success to my way of thinking is when the Lord comes. This is the ultimate success! When the Spirit takes possession of us as workers, the work accomplished will be of such a quality and of such magnitude that we will be in the same position as the New Testament church. They started out with their statistical records—3,000 souls, 5,000 souls. Then things got out of hand. The Apostolic General Conference Communications Department put several notices in their journal that read, "And believers were the more added to the Lord, multitudes both of men and women" (Acts 5:14). Another read, "And the word of God increased; and the number of the disciples multiplied in Jerusalem greatly; and a great company of the priests were obedient to the faith" (chap. 6:7). After these announcements, there are no more specific statistics relative to large numbers of baptisms in the book of Acts. They refer to membership additions by simply using the term *multitudes*.

Why don't we give less emphasis to numbers and statistics and more emphasis to the golden oil and see what happens? Only the Holy Spirit can produce this kind of success. Until that day, those filled with the golden oil will seek the highest standard of performance. We talk about expertise, skill, professionalism—but does not the Holy Spirit inspire a person to reach for the highest level of performance? In no way does a spiritual endowment lower the standards.

Ours is a spiritual work, to be accomplished by spiritual men and women, using the finest means and methods for the purpose of preparing a people spiritually to live with Christ forever. If this is not true, then why should we not hire the top public relations people in the world, whether they be atheist or Shintoist? Why not hire the finest public speakers to stand in our pulpits—men who are technical experts at persuading people even though they be agnostics? Why not hire Nobel-prize-winning scientists to teach in our schools, regardless of their beliefs and attitudes?

The wonderful thing about it all is that God takes common men and women and makes them uncommon through His Spirit. He takes fishermen and turns them into powerful witnesses for Him.

He takes men and women in this movement today and through His unlimited power uses them to carry His message of salvation to the lost multitudes.

"God's faithful messengers are to go steadily forward with their work. Clothed with the panoply of heaven, they are to advance fearlessly and victoriously, never ceasing their warfare until every soul within their reach shall have received the message of truth for this time."[8]

---

1   *Christ's Object Lessons,* p. 43.
2   *The Desire of Ages,* p. 362.
3   *Testimonies,* vol 7, pp. 158, 159.
4   *Ibid.,* vol. 9, p. 143.
5   *Evangelism,* p. 510.
6   *Temperance,* p. 232.
7   *Evangelism,* p. 682.
8   *Ibid.,* pp. 705, 706.

Chapter 22

Time for the Word

New titles on every conceivable spiritual subject pour from the presses daily. Books dealing with personality problems, social issues, and Christian biographies are going to be big, the forecasters tell us. Christian magazines (including *Ministry*) vie for our time and attention. The use of electronic media by the church is increasing rapidly. Can a busy pastor in today's fast-paced religious world keep current and still find time for the Word of God?

I approach such a question wondering, "What words or thoughts can I, a mere man, set forth regarding the place and position God and His Word should hold in the life? How can I do justice to the exalted, central focus the Scriptures must command if we are to be God's messengers faithfully proclaiming His Word to the world?" Increasing daily is my concern to understand God's will and to allow Christ to be Lord of my own life—a concern, incidentally, that reaches beyond my own church to the Christian world in general.

Frankly, much of what I hear, see, or read of Christian communication seems to have very limited value in establishing and increasing my relationship to God. I confess that most Madison Avenue religious telecasts, with their gorgeous props and polished appeals for financial support, all too often focus my mind on the histrionics rather than on Christ and His Word. During auto travels, I tune in the religious radio broadcasts, only to be harangued and not helped more often than not. Attempts to reach the world with the gospel are commendable, but what must serious-minded non-Christians think when they see and hear some of the programs that claim to preach the gospel? The emotional excitement, the search for something new and startling, and the excessive emphasis on feelings detract from the truth as it is in Jesus.

Let me illustrate. Recently, a letter written by a Christian lay leader in an African country came to my desk. He spoke of his experience in a religious organization that majored in emotional experiences. In his own words, "I came out of a vibrant church, alive with the speaking of tongues, miracles seen often, emotional singing, tears of joy filling the eyes of the congregation, prophesying and spiritual interpretations, people slain by the Spirit, and people dancing with the power of the Spirit—to name but a few manifestations."

Yet, in spite of this intense and seemingly gratifying spiritual adventure, his search for a deeper experience led him to attend a Bible seminar in which the emphasis was on Scripture. His heart was touched in a different way than ever before, resulting in a penetrating study of the Bible. During the past nine years, this man has spent two hours every day searching the Word, in spite of his many duties as a lay leader in the church.

Initially his previous diet of religious excitement left him feeling spiritually dead in his new program. It took several years before the Scriptures became a part of him, firmly establishing his relationship with God. He concluded his letter, "I have found calm and peace for my soul. Now my experience is based not on emotion, but on the words of the Bible—a 'Thus saith the Lord.'"

"Calm and peace" certainly must be considered an emotional experience. But notice that his experience of calmness and peace is a *product* of a faith solidly rooted in Scripture, not the *cause* of that faith. The gospel loses its dynamic power when the Scriptures are set aside or used as an adjunct to something else. To subordinate God's Word to feeling is as foolish as selecting a used car on the basis of soft seats rather than mechanical condition.

Because what a person believes controls what a person does, the contents of a church's message to the world must be given primary attention. The religious philosophies that have the strongest hold on the heart and mind are responsible for human attitudes and actions. Our character can never be elevated one iota above our concepts of truth and holiness. Our ideas of God mold our character. If we believe that God has neither love for nor interest in us, we will have little sincere regard for our fellow beings. Those who believe that the Holy Spirit has little or no influence on human behavior will certainly fail to experience His power in their own lives.

Jesus declared to the people in His day, "Ye do err, not knowing the scriptures" (Matt. 22:29). It is not coincidence that the decadent moral conditions in our society have paralleled to a large degree the weakened influence of the Bible, as it has been robbed of its power by being ignored, critically dissected, or completely rejected. When Israel elevated the Word of God by conforming to its commands, she prospered.

Our first business

The coming storm connected with the return of our Lord is upon us. Today is preparation time. Our first business as ministers must be to search the Scriptures diligently every day, not to prove a cherished point but to find out what God's will is and to order our lives accordingly. Ours cannot be an imaginary, fanciful religion of feeling or form; only a mighty cathedral of living truth based on the bedrock of the Bible is sufficient to control and guide our lives.

I am weary of hearing gimmicky sermons, philosophical frolicking, and repetitious twaddle. I want to hear the Word expounded, accompanied by a divine manifestation that brings sensitivity to the conscience and new life to the soul. Let me hear, not the superficial compliment of the untouched ("Oh, pastor, what a marvelous preacher you are!"), but rather, "Did not our hearts burn within us, while he talked with us by the way, and while he opened to us the scriptures?" (Luke 24:32).

To be sure, we have those in our pews who love to have their ears scratched. But could it be that there are some pulpits filled with Herods, who after their orations eagerly listen for the cry, "Is it the voice of a god, and not of a man?"

Preacher, remember, in every audience or congregation are many who sincerely cry out for the word of truth, for the presence of the living God in their lives. Don't feed them tradition, speculative theories, and specious interpretations, but rather let them hear the voice of the Eternal One speaking to them through your study of the Scriptures.

God has not preserved His Word through the centuries for us to ignore or misuse. His Word is a light, a two-edged sword, a fortress, a refuge, a hidden treasure, the good seed, an unerring guide, our richest heritage, an educator, a friend, food for soul, the rule of life, the foundation of our faith, the book above all books, the bread of life, our chart and compass, the alpha and omega of knowledge.

At the risk of sounding fanatical, I wonder what power would come into the church, what vibrant, active, witnessing, obedient Christians our members might become, if we spent 95 percent of our reading and study time with the Scriptures alone, and only 5 percent with all the rest of the religious literature pouring from the presses. If the truth were known, I suspect we would discover that presently these percentages are reversed for many of us. A thorough study of the Word will not necessarily exclude the reading of other religious material. But that reading material that diverts the mind from God and His Word must be laid aside.

In a Christian publication that came to my attention not long ago, one article featured a young man who, by his own estimation, has read some 800 science fiction books. He was once a Christian but has since left the church. Yet he emphatically denies that his reading habits are responsible, even partially, for his turning away from religion. One can hardly fail to wonder whether this young man would not still be part of the Christian body had he spent his time with the 66 books of Scripture rather than saturating his mind with science fiction.

Surely we can readily see that one of the major reasons why our world faces an overwhelming spiritual crisis is the woeful ignorance of the Scriptures prevailing today. In Old Testament times, God's messengers and prophets were often killed in an effort to silence their witness; today we can accomplish the same objective by ignoring their writings.

Isaiah's Messianic prophecy, "For behold, darkness shall cover the earth, and thick darkness the peoples; but the Lord will arise upon you, and his glory will be seen upon you" (Isa. 60:2, RSV; cf. chap. 9:1, 2), was fulfilled at the first coming of Christ. A dearth of spiritual discernment, accumulating for centuries, had reached its nadir. To a large degree, tradition had replaced the Scriptures. Required learning emphasized nonessentials and elevated external forms.

Word of life and light

From the realms of indescribable glory to the enveloping folds of darkest shadows Jesus came to dispel the gloom of misapprehension and misunderstanding regarding God. Speaking of the Christ, John says, "In him was life; and the life was the light of men. And the light shineth in darkness; and the darkness comprehended it not" (John 1:4, 5). Jesus Himself announced, "I am come a light into the world, that whosoever believeth on me should not abide in darkness (John 12:46). Christ was light to the people through His words and actions.

In His famous bread-of-life message (see John 6), He called upon His hearers to eat His flesh and drink His blood. Strange as it must have sounded in the ears of His hearers, He underlined the importance of His invitation by declaring that unless they ate His flesh and drank His blood, they could have no life now or for eternity. The message is clear. We receive His life by receiving His Word. "The words that I have spoken to you are spirit and life" (John 6:63, RSV).

The principle expressed in Hosea's day is still applicable today. "My people are destroyed for lack of knowledge; because you have rejected knowledge, I reject you from being a priest to me. And since you have forgotten the law of your God, I also will forget your children" (Hosea 4:6, RSV).

This is not an arbitrary act of God. It is the obvious result when one feeds one's mind on nonessentials, good as they may be, to the exclusion of a deep, thorough knowledge of the Scriptures.

A word of caution is in order here. Paul tells us that spiritual things are spiritually discerned (1 Cor. 2:14). It is possible to have a very intimate knowledge of the Bible, including the ability to read it in Hebrew and Greek, and yet not know the meaning of the Scriptures, or the Author of the Scriptures. Christ, as the Saviour of the world, stands as the key that unlocks both Old Testament and New Testament doors. Furthermore, if we do not have a constant dependence on the Holy Spirit to quicken our faculties, the Scriptures will remain a sealed book or, even worse, become twisted and garbled through our misunderstanding. A knowledge of truth depends on sincerity of purpose, not on the strength of our intellect. The great paradox of Scripture is that at the same time it is both profound and simple. The person of limited intellectual ability who approaches its study with an honest desire to learn God's will and a dependence on the Holy Spirit's aid will know more of truth than will the person of large mental capacity who comes to the Scriptures in his own strength and without a sense of its importance to his personal existence.

When we understand the grand purpose of Scripture and realize that through its pages our mind is brought into contact with the Infinite, we will covet every moment possible to spend in its study. We will consider our fellowship with the Eternal One through Bible study a privilege and honor—never drudgery.

Restoring God's image

Overshadowing all other appeals for making the Scriptures the center of our study life is the tremendous purpose for which God revealed Himself to the human race through His Word—the restoration of His image in the human soul. This restoration is the focus of every passage of Scripture. Thus it is that the key that unlocks the Bible is Jesus Christ, Author of the science of redemption.

Can the busy pastor keep current in the fast-paced religious world of today and still find time for the Word of God? I would submit that in no other way can the busy pastor of today remain current than by making the Word of God the center around which all else in his fast-paced life revolves. The Word alone provides the context by which he can assimilate and evaluate all else. Preacher friend, I appeal to you, as I appeal to myself: Make the Scriptures your constant companion; become known as a person of the Book; be utterly ruthless in uprooting nonessentials and carving time from your schedule for the study of God's Word; let it be common knowledge that here is the secret of your ministry.

To open the pages of the Bible is to be ushered into the presence of Him whom to know is life eternal. To open the pages of the Bible is to breathe, if only briefly, the rarefied atmosphere of heaven untainted by sin. To open the pages of the Bible is to see God's hand drawn aside, revealing vistas of a new and better world, a new and better life in which all that we have dreamed and hoped and longed for in our most exalted moments is seen as gloriously possible.

Chapter 23

And Remember— Jesus is Coming Soon!

[Spiritual to the core, Bob Spangler always turned to the Second Coming of Christ for an answer to life's disturbing questions. Nothing excited him, his preaching, or his ministry as much as Christ crucified, risen, and coming again. In the midst of life or death, joy or sorrow, despair or hope, he never failed to affirm God's ultimate dawn. Here are Bob's deep meditations on six great questions—Ed.]

Why do some righteous perish?

"The righteous perish, and no one takes it to heart; men of good faith are swept away, but no one cares, the righteous are swept away before the onset of evil, but they enter into peace; they have run a straight course and rest in their last beds" (Isa. 57:1, 2, NEB).

In the conflict between good and evil, one event has perplexed many a sincere soul. Why are faithful, devout Christians sometimes cut down in premature death? These deaths constitute not only a public loss but a church loss. The background of this text is found in the closing verses of Isaiah 56. The prophet speaks of the "beasts of the field" coming to devour God's people. This symbolizes the foreign nations that would attack Judah because of her sins. Yet God's watchmen, His ministers, were blind to this fact, and instead of warning people to repent and turn to God, they were shepherds with no understanding who turned to their own sinful ways.

The times in which these words were written were perilous, and the prophet declared that God in mercy permitted the death of certain of the righteous. In order that they might be delivered from great evils, they were laid to rest.

Perhaps the worst punishment God could have placed upon a sinner would be eternal life in our present world. Although death is regarded as an enemy, and so it is, many with a deep experience in the things of God do not fear it, and some even welcome it. The humiliation and sorrow of death are fully compensated by immortality at the glorious resurrection.

So when you see pious, useful, and talented Christians laid to rest, while some who are a problem to society and themselves—a cumberer of the ground— still live, do not question why. There could be two answers. The ones who live may be in need of more probationary time, and the ones who die will be spared sorrow, pain, and strife.

Our text declares that "the righteous perish, and no one takes it to heart."

There is One who always takes it to heart, and that is our Saviour. People may not care, but God always takes notice of the death of His people. So live today and every day in such a way that when death knocks at your heart's door you will have no fear of the Grim Reaper, for your life is hid with Christ in God.

Why be troubled?

"Let not your heart be troubled: ye believe in God, believe also in me. In my Father's house are many mansions: if it were not so, I would have told you. I go to prepare a place for you. And if I go and prepare a place for you, I will come again, and receive you unto myself: that where I am, there ye may be also" (John 14:1-3).

An elderly minister and his wife returned to her hometown on the banks of the Mississippi River for a visit. Familiar sights and sounds stirred many a memory in the woman's mind. Finally she turned to her husband and said, "Let's go down to the river and walk out on the old dock where I used to play and fish."

As they approached the dilapidated dock, no longer used as a boat stop, they noticed a boy about 12 years of age standing at the end with a suitcase beside him. After greeting him, they asked why he was standing there in the rain. He replied that he was waiting for a boat to stop and pick him up. Knowing that boats no longer stopped there, they invited him up to the old home place to wait until the rain subsided. The boy didn't say much, but insisted on staying there to meet the coming boat. Thinking that he would soon change his mind and not wanting to leave the child in the rain, the old couple stayed and sheltered him with their umbrellas. After a few moments they noticed in the distance a river steamer headed their way. To the amazement of the elderly pair, the boat pulled up alongside the dock and nearly stopped. Strong arms quickly reached out and pulled the boy and his suitcase on board. The boy, turning around as the steamer continued on, called back in a loud voice, "I knew the boat would come because my father is the captain!"

Our text is a familiar one. Do we really believe He will come again? Are these words a part of our lives?

"Let not your heart" refers to the seat of spiritual life and not our physical heart. But the fact is, believing in God and His Son affects the physical heart for the better!

It is such a marvelous thought to see, by faith, Christ actually preparing a place for us. This is an absolute, unchangeable fact. If it weren't, Christ would have told us so. He can only tell us truth! *He will come again.*

Can we be sure?

"Son of man, what is the proverb that you have about the land of Israel, saying, 'The days grow long, and every vision comes to nought'? Tell them therefore, 'Thus says the Lord God: I will put an end to this proverb, and they shall no more use it as a proverb in Israel.' But say to them, 'The days are at hand,

and the fulfillment of every vision'" (Eze. 12:22, 23, RSV).

Multitudes lived and died while hoping to see the first coming of the Lord. Old Mother Earth was wounded with the graves of billions, yet the Lord did not return. Finally a day came when a baby was born in Bethlehem. It was none other than the same God who breathed into Adam's nostrils the breath of life. His glory was locked in human flesh, but nevertheless He was the Lord. Few recognized Him as such. Several wise men and a few shepherds were among those who did. The unknown priest who held Jesus in his arms had no idea that he was holding the King of the universe, clothed in human garb. The only babies he recognized were those from wealthy homes.

He didn't know that he held the One whom Moses had asked to see His glory 1,500 years before. But here was the Lord who had come at last.

Can you imagine the delight of the disciples who believed in Him as the Messiah? They went through heartbreak and disappointment when they saw Him crucified. As they looked at the blood-streaked form of the One whom they believed was the Lord, their hopes were dashed. Feelings of horror and despair swept over their souls as they watched the soldiers stab a spear into the side of Christ. They returned home dejected and despondent, for their Lord was dead. But their dejection was turned into jubilation just a few hours later, when they realized He had risen from the dead. For 40 days they enjoyed His fellowship, and finally they strained their eyes to catch the last glimpse of Jesus as He ascended into the heavens. The words of the two angels burned hope into their hearts. "This same Jesus . . . shall so come in like manner as ye have seen him go" (Acts 1:11).

Some today may say that "every vision comes to nought," but the Lord declares, "The days are at hand, and the fulfillment of every vision." Jesus is coming soon.

Will you be there?

"We shall be changed. For this perishable nature must put on the imperishable, and this mortal nature must put on immortality" (1 Cor. 15:52-53, RSV). At the coming of Jesus the righteous will go through a mysterious but exhilarating experience. A new, perfect physical life will possess us. The mantle of immortality will be quietly but quickly slipped over the haggard bodies of the living saints.

Even at best, we today live in worn and jaded physical homes. Paul, describing his own feelings, says, "We groan, earnestly desiring to be clothed upon with our house which is from heaven" (2 Cor. 5:2). These bodies of ours have never known the thrill of immortality. Ah, but when the voice of Christ is heard, an instant metamorphosis takes place. We have been bound in cocoons of frailty, infirmity, and feebleness, but now we shall emerge in eternal vigor and health.

If the gospel offered nothing more than this experience, it would be worth everything to obey the Lord.

Think of defying gravity with no fear of falling. We rise to join the angelic parade and begin our trip to heavenly Zion. In living chariots of angels, we are rocketed to the third heaven. On our way home, we may spend some of the time pinching ourselves to make sure that we are actually leaving this earth to be with our Saviour. See in the distance a glorious light, greater than a billion aurora borealises of the Arctic. The brilliance of this light surpasses atomic explosions. Only immortal eyes can bear it. Word is passed around that it comes from the throne of God within the New Jerusalem. Our majestic train finally slows down and stops just outside the most magnificent walls ever beheld by human eyes. These are not fortifications, but foundations of beauty that delight the eye.

"What beauty and glory will meet the astonished sight of those who have seen no greater beauties in the earth than that which they beheld in decaying nature after the threefold curse was upon the earth."[1]

At last we have arrived in our eternal hometown, the New Jerusalem! Will you be there? This experience is yours through faith in the Lord Jesus Christ.

How will He come?

"Behold, he is coming with the clouds, and every eye will see him, every one who pierced him; and all tribes of the earth will wail on account of him. Even so. Amen" (Rev. 1:7, RSV). It is a familiar text, isn't it? Do you believe it will happen? Life's routine continues—people die, babies are born, mouths laugh, eyes cry. There is buying, selling, building, digging—on and on, life continues. We play the entire scale of human emotions.

Some faithful souls ask, "When will we cross over Jordan?" Others ask, "When will the words of promise from the two white-clad angels be fulfilled, "This same Jesus . . . shall so come in like manner?"

We cannot pinpoint the day or the hour when He will return, but someday soon God will jolt the steering wheel of this planet, sending it into mammoth convulsions of agony. It will be the midnight hour of the spiritual and physical darkness of this earth. Just as the visage of Christ was marred more than any person's, so the face of old Mother Earth will be mutilated and disfigured beyond recognition. It will be earth's Gethsemane, leading up to its final and complete crucifixion in the postmillennial purification fires. In this final scene of earth's torture, there will be two classes of people. The large group will beg for mercy as they shout for the rocks and mountains to fall on them. But the other group, with faces turned heavenward during these awful moments, will search the sky for the arrival of the Son of God! In the distance they will see the small cloud the size of a human hand, as Ellen White describes it. On the royal highway of the skies the celestial caravan of the Lord of hosts will roll toward the earth. The same angels that sang over Bethlehem's hills, announcing Christ's first coming, will be at the head of this mighty parade.

Oh, what feelings will be ours if saved! A description of the sight, sound, and emotions of this event is impossible. The important thing is to be ready to meet our Lord, with our sins forgiven and our lives patterned after His. Let the coming of Christ be uppermost in your mind today and every day of your existence. What glory it will be when we shall meet Him in the clouds of the heavens!

When will He come?

"Hold yourselves ready, therefore, because the Son of Man will come at the time you least expect him" (Matt. 24:44, NEB).

Often I've been asked the question, What do you consider to be the signs most indicative of Christ's soon return? Another question I am frequently asked is, When do you think Christ will come? Will it be A.D. 2000 or before? There is no doubt in my mind that social, political, and economical events are reaching crisis proportions that will culminate in the Second Coming of Christ. But even more than these calamitous crises I see two indicators of a more positive nature that herald the soon return of our Lord.

First, I have witnessed firsthand the rapid spread of the gospel in every part of the world. It is encouraging to find that thousands are committing their lives fully to Christ in such countries as Korea, India, South America, Africa, and Russia.

Second, I see an unprecedented spiritual renewal on the part of a great many individuals. There is an earnestness, a longing in the hearts of many, young and old alike, to secure and maintain a close relationship with Christ. This new awareness points to the nearness of the Second Advent.

That brings me to the question of A.D. 2000. Some are convinced that the coming of the bimillennial will complete the 6,000 years of our world's history. Frankly, I feel that it is not wise to set any particular point of time for our Lord's return. Our attention should not be focused on time as much as on faithful preparation for His return and on an active participation in letting the world know of the nearness of this great event. To the discerning Christian, conditions such as disintegrating morals, economic crises, political problems, energy depletion, and pollution are merely signposts along the way.

Such Christians heed the Saviour's command found in Luke 21:28: "And when these things begin to come to pass, then look up, and lift up your heads; for your redemption draweth nigh."

The important question we should ask ourselves is, Am I ready to meet my Lord whether it be twenty-five, fifty, or one hundred years from now? His return could come *before* A.D. 2000! Why not? Remember, Jesus is coming soon! "Even so, come, Lord Jesus" (Rev. 22:20).

---

1   *Spiritual Gifts*, vol. 3, pp. 88, 89.